!

!!

A Short Introduction
to the
Philosophy of Śāntarakṣita

A Short Introduction to the Philosophy of Śāntarakṣita

Marie-Louise Friquegnon

William Paterson University

coolgrovepress - a zangdokpalri edition

First published and in print in the United States by
Coolgrove Press, an imprint of Cool Grove Publishing, Inc. New York.
512 Argyle Road, Brooklyn, NY 11218
All rights reserved under the International and
Pan-American Copyright Conventions.

www.coolgrove.com

For permissions and other inquiries please visit coolgrove.com

ISBN-13: 978-1482317459

ISBN-10: 1482317451

Author's acknowledgements
I wish to thank my teachers, Khenchen Palden Sherab Rinpoche and
Khentrul Tsewang Dongyal Rinpoche for their guidance in writing this
book. I also thank my husband Raziel Abelson for proofreading the
manuscript and for his invaluable suggestions throughout, and my
publisher Tej Hazarika, for his patience, diligence and support.

Front cover painting by Phurba Namgay

With the exception of the cover, all Sanskrit words
will be written the way they are pronounced.

Printed and bound in the USA * Amazon.com Edition.

Dedicated to my teachers,
Khenchen Palden Sherab Rinpoche,
Khentrul Tsewang Dongyal Rinpoche and
Raziel Abelson.

Table of Contents

PREFACE

The first time I read Shantarakshita's philosophy was in 1982 when I first discovered the *Tattvasamgraha*. I was immediately fascinated by this work which seemed to point towards a synthesis of so many of the insights of my favorite philosophers. When Khenchen Palden Sherab Rinpoche and Khentrul Tsewang Dongyal Rinpoche told me about Shantarakshita's *Madhyamakalankara* (*The Ornament of the Middle Way*) and the *Tattvasiddhi* (*The Attainment of Suchness*), I prevailed on them to help me put them into English, as well as their commentaries. This book began as a lengthy introduction to their work, which I thought better to publish separately. I am grateful to them for allowing me to use this material, and to quote from the yet unpublished translations forthcoming in Robert Thurman's series at Columbia University Press. I also wish to thank the late Prof. Virgil Aldrich, Prof. Hyun Hochsmann, Geshe Lozang Jamspal, Prof. John O'Connor, Prof. Richard Rumana, Prof Eric Steinhart, and the late Prof. Ninian Smart for reading the earlier version, Toy Tung, Nathalie Hauptman and Beth Wilber for their editorial help and criticism, Katherine Brown, Noé Dinnerstein, Brian Fanning, Claudia Geers, Joan Remy, John Paul Gorgoroso and Peter Tung for their technical assistance, and William Paterson University for its support during this project. I am grateful to the original publishers, Wadsworth Press, for giving me back the rights to their edition of this work, On Shantarakshita. Most of all I wish to thank my husband, Raziel Abelson for his indispensable help and patience. Although this study is very limited in scope, I hope it will inspire scholars to a further exploration of the work of Shantarakshita.

I refer throughout to James Blumenthal. *The Ornament of the Middle Way.* Ithaca: Snow Lion, 20004

Jamgon Mipham. *The Adornment of the Middle Way.* Padmakara Translation Group. Boston: Shambhala, 2005

Ju Mipham *Speech of Delight* Trans. Thomas Doctor. Ithaca: Snow Lion, 2004.

List of Abbreviations

KR	Kenchen Palden Sherab Rinpoche's oral teaching
JBy	dbU ma rgyan gyi brjed byang (by Je Tsong Khapa)
MA	Madhyamakalamkara
MAV	Madhyamakalamkaravritti
MAP	Madhyamakalamkarapanjika
TS	Tattvasamgraha
TSP	Tattvasamgrahapanjika
TATTVA	Tattvasiddhi
MAV	Madhyamakalankaravritti

Khenpo Shantarakshita

INTRODUCTION

THE LIFE OF SHANTARAKSHITA

Sometimes in a philosophical tradition a figure appears that stands as the culmination of what has gone before. Many would choose as such figures Aristotle, Averroes, Maimonides, St. Thomas Aquinas, Kant, and Bertrand Russell. In the Buddhist tradition, I would designate Shantarakshita for this role. An expert on non-Buddhist as well as Buddhist schools of thought, he was critical of all of them, yet not nihilistic. Like Kant, he held the phenomenal level to be of the nature of mind, only relatively true, while affirming the absolute level to be real, yet unknowable through our conceptual understanding. He believed that non-conceptual awareness of the absolute was possible through meditation, and that it provides us with an experience that enriches our lives with wisdom, compassion and bliss.

Shantarakshita was born in Bengal, the son of the king. The date of his birth is uncertain, but we know for sure that he was teaching philosophy at the monastic university of Nalanda and in Tibet in the eighth century CE. It is said that he lived a very long time. He knew of the work of Santideva, another important figure in Tibetan Buddhist philosophy, who also taught at Nalanda University. He quotes from Santideva's *Bodhicharyavatara* in the *Tattvasiddhi*. He was gifted in philosophy from childhood. A professor at Nalanda, he became head of the university. He studied with the philosopher Jnanagarbha, and received monastic vows from him. He combined philosophic brilliance with intense religious devotion, particularly to the buddha of wisdom, Manjushri. He traveled widely, teaching in Nepal, China and East Turkistan (Liyul), and perhaps in Korea and Japan. He is most famous for his introduction of philosophical Buddhism to Tibet.

Tibetans had been familiar with Buddhist ideas since the reign of the thirty-third king of Tibet, Srongtsan Gampo (*Srong-btsan-sgam-po*). As a result of his successful military campaigns in Nepal and China, he was able to demand Nepalese and Chinese princesses as brides. Both these princesses were devout Buddhists, and together they influenced their husband.

Although the successors of Srongstan Gampo were sympathetic to Buddhism, the first openly committed king was Thrisrong Detsen (*Khri-gtsrong lde-btsan*). the thirty-eighth king of Tibet who ascended the throne at the age of seventeen (Dongyal, 1999). After waging many wars, and extending the boundaries of Tibet, he became very interested in Buddhism. He sent investigators to find the perfect Buddhist master. They searched throughout India, China and Nepal. Finally Bargyalwai Lodro (rBar gyalbai blo gros) found Shantarakshita, who was teaching at Nalanda.

Buddhist philosophy predominated at Nalanda, and its scholars debated freely with proponents of a dozen other traditions. In addition, Buddhists philosophers of different persuasions debated freely with each other, rivaling each other in their standards of clarity, precision and insight.

When told about Shantarakshita, the king was delighted and sent eight emissaries, two at a time, carrying gold for him. The pairs of emissaries kept two miles apart, because there were so many robbers. Six reached Shantarakshita and asked him to come to Tibet for the ground-breaking of their new temple. Although he was very advanced in age, he agreed to go.

As Shantarakshita approached the city of Lhasa, King Thrisrong Detsen came to meet him. The king asked him what his doctrine was. He replied, "To believe what is in accordance with reason, and to reject what is not in accordance with reason." Then they traveled together to the place where Samye university/monastery would be built. Shantarakshita laid out the architectural plan in accordance with that of the Otentpari monastery in India. Unfortunately, at that time, there were a number of unusual natural disasters such as floods, storms, earthquake and avalanches, and the native Bonpo priests blamed them on the introduction of the foreign religion of Buddhism. They insisted that Shantarakshita leave the country. (Dongyal, 1999)

Buddhism was still resisted by the masses, and by many nobles as well. This was partly because of political reasons. Buddhism was a peace-loving religion, and the Tibetans had been doing very well with their war-like ways. It was also a foreign religion, and the people feared domination by China or India. They also resented having to care for so many foreign monks. Tibetan conquests had caused so much upheaval, particularly in China and Nepal, that, ironically, monks were forced to go to Tibet to seek refuge with its Buddhist king.(Snellgrove, 1987, p. 381) Finally, the people were afraid that the foreign religion would anger the local gods and demons, and that misfortunes such as smallpox (a very real danger with the foreign influx) and famine would beset the land.

Shantarakshita agreed to leave. This gentle scholar was suited for philosophical debates, not confrontations with demons and shamans. He advised the king to invite the great tantric Buddhist master Guru Padmasambhava to subdue the Bonpo. What followed was a contest between magicians reminiscent of Moses' struggle with the Egyptian priests. The problem was solved, and so Shantarakshita returned to Tibet. The monastery university was built. He established a school of philosophy, renowned for translators, in order that the entire compendium of Buddhist and non-Buddhist philosophical and religious studies of India could be read in Tibetan. Eventually there were more than a thousand translators working at Samye.

Shantarakshita was famous for his kindness as well as his brilliance. It is said that he won the affection of the people by praising their tea, which was made by boiling water with tea, salt and yak butter. He was also called Bodhisattva.

Beginning his instruction with seven young students, all of whom became great scholars, he put scholarship and philosophical analysis on a firm foundation in Tibet. In the brief period before his death, he built a network of monastic colleges and trained a generation of philosophers, teachers and translators. Like St. Thomas Aquinas among Christians and Shankara among Hindus, Shantarakshita is regarded as a saint by many Buddhists. Some regard him as an emanation of Buddha Vajrapani. His style of writ-

3

ing is full of good humor and charm. As described by Dr. B. Bhattacharya:

"He advances his arguments slowly and confidently, but with extraordinary caution, and with examples considered valid by both parties, anticipating objections which may be put forward by his antagonist at every step. These objections he nullifies as objections arise, and ultimately smashes each and every argument on which the theories of his opponent are based, and drives his adversary to a corner. He then explains to his opponent what his position is tantamount to, and proves that the only way to escape from this undesirable position is to hold a Buddhist theory or be a Buddhist. On such occasions Shantarakshita is as jovial as a child and from his mouth flow examples of the best kind of humour associated with a refined dignity. His humour is seen very frequently when his opponent is driven by his arguments to a theory which is an accepted fact in Buddhism." (Bhattacharya, 1984. p. xiv)

Kamilasila, who provides us with an extensive commentary to Shantarakshita's *Tattvasamgraha*, was an important philosopher in his own right. Having been Shantarakshita's student at Nalanda, he was invited to Tibet by King Thrisrong Detsen. He arrived there after the death of Shantarakshita. The king was concerned about the teachings of the Chinese monk Mo-ho-yen (Hoshang Mahayana), who was arguing that, to be perfectly still, without thought, was all that was needed for enlightenment. Kamalashila replied that without the active participation of the mind, emptiness cannot be realized. Further, if one tries to suppress thought, one is saddled with the thought that one needs to suppress thought. Only through discriminating thought, i.e. philosophy, and also through meditation, can one achieve enlightenment. Kamalashila won a debate against the Chinese teacher, and the Indian tradition of Shantarakshita became the dominant philosophy in Tibet.

Shantarakshita usually does not provide us with the names of his opponents, but only with their arguments. Kamalashila fills in the names, quotes from their works, and extends the arguments.

Shantarakshita's place of birth is uncertain, but he was probably born about 713. Bhattacharya gives Shantarakshita's, dates as 705-762, but there is a great deal of disagreement about this. (Bhattacharya, 1984 foreward)

Note:

Bhattacharya, B foreward to *Tattvasamgraha* of Shantarakshita Baroda Oriental Institute, 1984

CHAPTER 1

Buddhism and Philosophy

Is Buddhism a religion or a philosophy? It does not seem to require faith of its followers. Sakyamuni Buddha asked that his disciples not accept anything as true just because he had said it, and that one should test the truth of what he said as a goldsmith tests gold to see if it is pure. There is no belief in a creator of the universe. People are asked to liberate themselves rather than to rely on an external source of help.

Buddhism, however, is unlike philosophy because it does not encourage indulging in speculation about questions that seem unanswerable. There is no time, Buddha said, because the need to escape suffering for oneself and others is so urgent. In an early text a young man named Malunkyaputta, decides to leave the monastic life unless Buddha answers questions for him about the origin of the universe, the truth about reincarnation, whether or not the soul and body are the same, etc. Buddha replies that one would die before one could find an answer to such questions. He says that if a man is struck by an arrow, and refuses to have it taken out until he learns who shot it, what caste and color the person was, and so forth, he would die before he was treated. Similarly, immersed in samsara as we are, on death row, not knowing the time or manner of our inevitable death, we must spend our time achieving the transformation of mind that will lead us to nirvana. (Burtt 1955, p.32-36)

The way to accomplish this, Buddha said, was to recognize the validity of the four noble truths and to follow the eightfold path. The four noble truths are modeled on the ancient questions an

6

Aryuvedic physician would ask when treating a patient. What is the disease? What is its cause? Can the cause be removed and the patient cured? How can this be done? Buddha's answer was that the disease is suffering, the cause is mental, - dissatisfaction or craving, and that this can be overcome by following the eightfold path. This path necessitates accepting the four noble truths, committing oneself to the path, using one's speech in a positive manner, having good moral conduct such as not killing, stealing, lying, misusing sex or becoming intoxicated, having a livelihood consistent with compassion, making a concerted effort to follow this path, reflecting on the nature of suffering and meditating. The nature of suffering is traced to impermanence. No matter how hard we try, we cannot hold on to the things we cherish. At every moment, all things, even those that seem the most stable, are withering away. On reflection, even our cherished selves change all the time. Our supposed independence from one another is an illusion. Everything interacts with everything else. This is the Buddhist refutation of philosophical egoism. We need to care about others as ourselves for there are no real boundaries between self and other. Concepts about individual things are imposed on reality by the mind. Our knowledge is relative to our point of view. Liberation consists in freeing that point of view from suffering.

So far, this sounds only like a philosophy of life. Where is the religious aspect? It comes I believe within meditation, that is, within experience rather than logic, experience and logic being the two pillars on which Buddhism is founded. There are two aspects of meditation in Buddhism, *samatha* (calming the mind) and *vipasyana* (insight). When the mind is calm, there may arise in it an insight that cannot be put into words. It brings great joy that eventually cannot be disturbed by anything that happens. It is associated with wisdom and compassion. It is similar to the reports of the experiences of God or the Absolute by mystics in other religious traditions. Thomas Merton, the great Catholic Benedictine monk, reflected that there seemed to him to be no difference between his contemplative experience of God and what he experienced in Buddhist meditation.

To return to the place of philosophy in Buddhism, one might well ask if Buddha was so reluctant to engage in philosophical debate, why are there libraries full of Buddhist philosophy? The answer, I believe, was that it became a necessity, because Buddhists were constantly being challenged, particularly by the great Hindu and Jain philosophers of the ancient and medieval periods. According to Prof. Robert Thurman (in a lecture at Columbia University) Buddhists began writing down their teachings in the vernacular, at a time when Hindus thought their sacred texts ought only to be transmitted orally by Brahmins in Sanskrit. It was the Buddhist rejection of the caste system that led so many of the merchant caste to become converts. These merchants used writing more than anyone else, because of commercial requirements. Once people began reading Buddhist texts in Pali, Hindus began to write theirs down in Sanskrit. When Buddhist ideas were under attack, Buddhist thinkers had to respond. So they too began to write in Sanskrit, which was a sort of a *lingua franca*. Debates began to be staged at the great Indian monastery universities. These were taken very seriously. Sometimes the king was present, and the disputants were often under binding agreement to have the whole university convert to the views of a successful debater.

As time went on, Buddhist philosophers took varying views on classic philosophical questions, such as the nature of reality and knowledge. Some were atomists, identifying the material world with the ever-changing interaction of unchanging atoms. Others, idealists, identified reality with a universal ever changing mind.

The Madhyamaka (middle way) philosopher, Nagarjuna, returning to the Buddha's reluctance to take a philosophical position, believed that attachment to a belief in anything permanent and substantial was an impediment to enlightenment. (Nargarjuna, 1995). He believed that it was intellectual folly to have such an attachment. In a series of arguments reminiscent of Zeno, he laid the foundation for the Madhyamaka school which divided reality into the absolute and relative level. Madhyamaka means the middle way, because the purpose of the school was to steer a middle ground between eternalism (the belief that we can know eternal and unchanging entities) and nihilism (the belief that there is no veridical awareness whatever). On the relative level there is cause and effect, and one can make use of Buddhist practices to reach enlightenment. But these are just skillful means that help one to wake up from the dreams of relative reality. When one examines knowledge of the relative carefully, one discovers it is full of para-doxes. Absolute reality transcends thought and can only be known through meditation.

Shantarakshita and Philosophy: Shantarakshita's Philosophical Heritage

Philosophy in India at the time of Shantarakshita was divided up into the orthodox Hindu schools and the non-orthodox schools such as the Carvakas, the Jains and the Buddhists.

The Six Orthodox Schools

There were six orthodox schools. The Samkhyas believed in an all-pervading substance called *prakriti* or nature that formed the basis of everything. Although unitary, *prakriti* was said to contain three *gunas,* or qualities; *tejas* (brightness) associated with intellect, *rajas* (energy) and *tamas* (mass), and to prompt the formation of a con-scious individual self, the *purusha,* which was passive, and tended to be energized by *tejas.* This produced suffering. The way to lib-eration (*moksha*) was to disentangle the *purusha* from the *gunas.* This could be accomplished by cultivating non-attachment. In addition, one of the ways to do this was to practice certain yogic techniques. If *moksha* was achieved, then the *purusha* would remain in a state of peace forever. The Samkhya, like all the orthodox schools except the Mimamsa, believed that universes develop, degenerate and come to an end. Then a new universe comes from the ashes of the old.

The Samkhyas, although originally non-theistic, believed that *prakriti* itself had a teleological thrust. It provided everything the *purusha* needed throughout its lifetimes to eventually reach *moksha.* Shantarakshita argued against both theistic and non-theistic Samkhya.

The Yoga School, from the Sanskrit root "*yug*", to bind, had the same metaphysics as the Samkhya, (not to be confused with yoga in general which was practiced by many systems), but was theistic.

Moksha consisted in becoming close to God. They practiced various forms of yoga to purify the subtle body, a refined body existing within the regular body, so that a saving insight into the nature of being could be achieved, and union with God could be possible. As with the Samkhya system, the *purusha* that reached *moksha* would abide in eternal blissfulness.

The subtle body was believed to be in a way dissolved within the normal or gross body, but not so completely dissolved that it was inseparable. At death it could move into another gross body. The subtle body had material characteristics, but was very refined, and unobservable by ordinary means. It could be perceived through yogic perception. It was the abode of the *chakras*, centers of power, as well as channels of energy that were connected to them. Certain practices such as physical exercise, diet, control of the breathing as well as visualizing deities and having devotion to them, could purify these channels and open the "third eye" of yogic perception.

The Nyaya (logic) school, and the Vaishesika (to look for specific differences) school merged at a very early date. The Nyaya school, famous for its logical arguments, believed in a creator God. They believed each person had a soul and a body. But the soul was so abstract that although it persisted beyond death, it existed afterwards in such a qualityless way that the school was sometimes thought to believe in annihilation after death. They were known for a proof of the existence of God similar to that of William Paley's "The Watch and the Watchmaker". They said that if one found a pot, never having found one before, since it is so perfectly formed to hold water, one must conclude there is a pot maker. Similarly, since the universe is so orderly, it must have a maker.

The Vaishesika mainly contributed the view that all things were material, composed of atoms that were thought of as indivisible, as partless. A problem arose as to how these indivisible atoms could combine to form anything else. The Indian philosophers were familiar with zero (*sunya*), the only number that is indivisible. So it seemed as though the atom had an extension of zero. But since zero plus zero equals zero, it was not clear how these atoms could ever be combined to form objects with extensions greater than zero. So the Vaishesikas thought there must be a God who miraculously produced a quantum jump so that the atoms could combine to form an object of positive size.

The Mimamsa school is unlike all the other orthodox schools, because it holds the universe to be one and eternal. This is because the *Vedas*, residing in the universe and themselves eternal, must have an eternal repository. The Mimamsas are mainly concerned with rituals as described in the Vedas, which they believe to be effi-cacious in ensuring prosperity, quite independently of the exis-tence of God. Since their aim was to give a consistent account of the Vedas, they developed logic and became associated with the Nyaya. They believed in an eternal self that is a subject of experi-ence and the explanation for the continuity of memory. They had little interest in yoga or meditation, believing only that if one fol-lowed the directives found in the Vedas, one would go to a heav-enly realm after death.

The Mimamsa school produced the great seventh century philoso-pher Kumarila Bhatta, whose ideas about the existence of perma-nent individual selves were challenged by Shantarakshita.

The Vedanta (end or purpose of the Vedas) school, although the most influential in Hinduism, only achieved great importance after the time of Shantarakshita. The short life of Shankara, its most important figure, was probably in the late seventh or early eighth century. Shankara, like Descartes long after, believed it was impos-sible to doubt the existence of the self. For one needs a self to doubt the self. Further, the self is subject. To make it into an object is to falsify it. Thus the self is beyond conception. And one discovers through religious experience that it is Brahman or God. Brahman is, on the absolute level, everything that is. One cannot character-ize Brahman in words. It is *nirgunam*, without qualities. One knows the world in the ordinary, or relative sense as dualistic, shrouded by the veil of *maya*, that is, in an illusory way. On the rel-ative level, God appears for Hindus, as Vishnu, Siva etc. as Brahman *sagunam*, the Lord with qualities. Shankara, as well as

Gaudapada, his *paramaguru* or highest teacher, borrowed a great deal of their conceptual systems from late Buddhist thought. All Shantarakshita seems to have known of this school is that they believed all things to be in reality Brahman, which could be spoken of as *saccidananda*; being, consciousness and bliss. I will return to Shankara later in this study.

(Ramanuja, who lived some time in the eleventh century, adopted some of Shantarakshita's arguments against proofs for the existence of God, although he accepted God's existence without proof. He is famous for his defense of the independent existence of selves from God, while at the same time maintaining that selves and the universe were the body of God and that God was the mind or soul of the universe. Ramanuja,1966, pp. 161-174)

Non-Orthodox Indian Schools at the
Time of Shantarakshita

The Carvaka school shared the fate of materialist schools in the west , such as that of Democritus. Although Democritus wrote as much as Aristotle only fragments are left. This is also true of the Carvaka. Most people do not like atheistic, materialistic, deterministic systems very much so they do not bother to preserve them. In general, the Carvaka school only accepted as real those things that were perceptible. Their views were similar to those of David Hume and the logical positivists. Some Carvakas believed in atoms, but others rejected them because they could not be perceived. They denied the validity of inference, because it could be used to infer the existence of imperceptible beings. For example, the Nyaya Vaishesikas inferred the existence of God from the appearance of order in the universe. The Carvakas also rejected the belief that morality is objective. They were associated with immorality, but they may just have had bad press. Their view of life could be characterized as 'live, drink and be merry, for tomorrow we die.'

The Jains were a religion traditionally said to be founded by Mahavira, a bit earlier than Buddhism. Buddha studied with two Jain teachers. The Jains believed in the existence of individual souls and bodies. Suffering occurred because the soul was entangled in material attachments. Liberation consisted in removing this soul (*purusha*) gradually from attachment to the body through a series of rigorous ascetic practices. Finally, at the end of this process, the ascetic would practice ritual starvation (with the permission of the teacher). The soul would then achieve *moksha* and dwell forever in a state of happiness. The Jains were interested in both logic and philosophy. They were epistemological skeptics, believing one could know something only from a particular point of view, and that assertions about anything were always subject to doubt.[*]

Shantarakshita and the Origins of Buddhist Philosophy in Tibet

Tibet offers many gifts to the world. Her culture is rich in painting, sculpture, architecture and dance. Her people are skilled in many crafts, and are peace loving, warm and energetic. But Tibet's greatest gift is her philosophical tradition, a tradition which is only in this century becoming known in the west. A continuation of classical Indian metaphysics and logic, it encompasses all of the vehicles of Buddhism, and adds to them its own insights and explanations

Even a brief acquaintance with Tibetan thought shows that as early as the eighth century Tibetan scholars were very familiar with aspects of philosophy which would not be discovered in the west until Descartes. But of course, it is not important that the Tibetans thought of these things first. What is important is that they thought of them so well, so rigorously, and with a sensitive understanding of the merits of many different philosophic visions of the world.

Tibet never forgot her debt to India, the home of Sakyamuni, and the source of Madhyamaka philosophy. This philosophy exemplifies the uniqueness of Buddhism. For it states that all forms, i.e., all

---

[*] For an extended study of the various Indian Schools see Ninian Smart "Indian Philosophy" in the *Encyclopedia of Philosophy* ed. Paul Edwards New York: Macmillan,1967 and Bina Gupta *An Introduction to Indian Philosophy* New York: Routledge, 2012.

that we know, are empty in nature. That is, reality transcends our ability to describe it in words, to know it through conceptual understanding. Even the words of the Buddha are ultimately empty. Yet the understanding that is beyond conception is made accessible to us by them as a finger points to the moon. In this way, Buddhism avoids religious superstition, while also avoiding a hopelessly nihilistic and skeptical attitude. It was Indian scholars who brought these views to Tibet, along with their meditation skills and religious practices. Shantarakshita was the first among them.

According to Tibetans, they have actually invented nothing of their conceptual system. It is all implicit in the original *dharma* (teaching) of Sakyamuni Buddha. But the Buddha unveiled his teachings to suit the circumstances and abilities of practitioners, and these teachings continued to be revealed throughout his lifetime. He first preached what seemed essentially an empiricist philosophy, epistemologically and metaphysically similar to the view of David Hume. But whereas Hume suggested at the end of the Treatise that if one were disturbed by his findings one should not fret but have a game of billiards, Buddhists suggested certain practical ways of implementing their theories in order to bring about the good of all sentient beings.

According to Tibetan sources, Buddha Sakyamuni was born around 600 B.C. in Kapilavastu in Northern India. Named Siddharta Gautama, he was the son of the king of the Sakyas, at that time, India's most powerful king. His father was King Suddhadana, his mother, Queen Mayadevi. There were many special auspicious circumstances surrounding his birth. It was predicted that he would become either a great king or a great teacher.

Prince Siddhartha was very wise and compassionate by nature. From the age of eight he was educated in the sixty four kingly pursuits such as martial arts, horse racing, and archery. This education was completed at the age of twenty. Then he married Princess Yasodhara. Because at his birth it was predicted that he would be either a great teacher or a great king, he was sheltered by his father from any knowledge of old age, illness and death, in the hope that he would see no need to help others through his teachings, and would instead be a king.

Upon visiting three parks, south west and east, the boy encountered a sick pregnant woman, an old person and a corpse. His charioteer told him such things happen to everybody. Sickened by suffering, he visited a fourth park in the north and encountered a meditating monk. He questioned him and decided this was the path he should follow. Years before, at the age of eight his father had found him meditating under a tree. No matter where the sun was in the sky, the tree shaded him. Remembering this meditation, Siddhartha left his kingdom at the age of twenty-nine to live as a hermit. He studied with Jain and Hindu teachers but remained unsatisfied. (Dongyal, 1999)

There were many different theories among Hindus as to what constitutes liberation. The young Buddha fell in with a group of ascetics who believed that by denying the needs of the body, one could liberate the spirit. Probably some of them were influenced by Upanishadic tradition which denied the real existence of an individual self but believed, rather, in a sort of world soul which constitutes the real identity of all beings. Materialistic concerns block the realization of this identity and cause suffering so, by denying the body, the mind can merge into this world soul and achieve liberation.

Hence the Buddha fasted for six years. So great were his austerities that he nearly died. Yet he felt no closer to liberation than before. So he ended his fast, sat down under a tree and resolved not to get up until he had figured out the solution to the problem of suffering.

The Buddha then, viewing humanity as suffering from a disease, envisioned the cure in the following way. 1. The disease is suffering. 2. There would be no suffering if one were not attached to the things of this world such as riches, sexual pleasure, health, long life, etc. Craving, therefore, is the cause of suffering. 3. Suffering can be cured if this attachment or craving is eliminated. 4. The way to eliminate craving is two fold: a) wisdom, by understanding the cause of suffering and b) leading one's life in a manner that is calculated to bring about an end to craving. Basically, this involves good moral conduct, compassion and meditation.

This seems rather close to the Stoic ideal. Want nothing, and you will be satisfied with whatever you have. So you won't suffer. But if this were the end of the story, then Nietzsche's objection to Buddhism would make a lot of sense. Why prefer a guaranteed absence of suffering over the possibility of ecstasy even if the latter allows for the greater possibility of suffering? Life with all its excitement and ups and downs seems so much more of a challenge to the adventurous mind than a sort of lukewarm security.

But here the story of Buddhism really gets interesting. What occurs with the cessation of craving is not a neutral state of freedom from pain but an extremely ecstatic state that has been called absolute bliss, joy, understanding, perfection beyond words. What is the explanation for this? The answer does not seem to be given by early Buddhist thinkers but appears much later. The final answer appears in Shantarakshita's *Tattvasiddhi*, (*The Attainment of Suchness*). (Santaraksita's *Tattvasiddhi*, forthcoming)

Early Buddhists believed in the reality of the physical world, but not in the real nature of things as we perceive them. Tables, trees, humans, etc., are known through the senses which are internal to the body and subjective. The causes of these sensations, are atoms, indisible particles. One school, the Vaibhasika believed that objects composed of atoms were known directly, for example, as in the case of visual perception, a ray of light went out to the object and returned with a bit of it (the 'fish hook' theory of perception.) Others, The Sautrantikas, believed atoms were the causes of images which are our objects of knowledge. Although atoms could be said to exist, their nature was beyond conception.
There could be no soul, or permanent self either, for mind was not thought of as a special substance existing in a spiritual realm, but merely a sixth sense. Persons were in the same natural hodge podge as everything else and were constructions of mind just like tables and trees.
Nevertheless, early Buddhists (such as the *Sravakayanas*) did think

about liberation as personal. Only upon reaching nirvana was individuality snuffed out. So it was considered a good thing to enter into the kind of monastic life in which one disassociates one-self from the rest of the world. It is true, they thought, that one must practice compassion towards others, but this is to break the sense of self, so that craving can be extinguished. One's ultimate concern is one's own personal salvation.

But the quest for personal salvation raises a central philosophical issue. If "self" as a separate entity is merely a mental construction, then the liberation of such a self must be incomplete unless all such "selves" are liberated. Yet it seems an impossible task to liberate all beings. So how can anyone be liberated at all?

The answer to this question took many centuries to work out, and forms the nexus of the philosophical concern of the later schools of Mahayana Buddhism. There was no one answer to this question of ego clinging; rather, there were many answers, each of which gave rise to further questions, prompting a refinement of the view.

The method by which both the early and late Buddhists strove to reach enlightenment is called the eight fold path. This path is explained in different ways according to the various forms of Buddhism. The path includes right aspiration, right view, right livelihood, right speech, right conduct, right effort, right wisdom and right meditation. Lay people take vows to abstain from killing, stealing, lying, intoxication and sexual misconduct. Monks and nuns take vows of poverty and celibacy as well. Early Buddhists generally believed that one was not likely to reach nirvana if one did not take monastic vows. They reasoned it was too difficult to break all craving and attachments if one were entrenched in romantic relationships and the necessity of earning a living.

But as a result there were not very many people actively pursuing enlightenment. It was too difficult to renounce so much and many people found it both impractical and contrary to compassion to abandon their dependents. Later, Buddhism developed a two fold way of opening the path to all. The first aspect was connected with the doctrine of reincarnation and the requirement of universal salvation. Buddhas and *bodhisattvas*, chose not to remain in an isolated form of bliss, but took rebirth voluntarily for the sake of others. Through their extraordinary insight, wisdom and power they were able to inspire others to renounce attachments and follow the eight fold path. With their help, liberation became far easier to achieve. Secondly, the metaphysical system of later Mahayana, in its idealist and semi-idealist forms, stressed the primacy of mind in the formation of an experience. Renunciation, then, could be an act of mental detachment, while the devotee remained in the world, often actively engaged in raising a family and earning a living. An old Buddhist tale illustrates the change in attitude. Two monks were traveling together. They came to a wild river which they could cross, but with difficulty. A young woman was also trying unsuccessfully to cross. One monk, obeying the *vinaya* rules of discipline, did not even look at her. The other picked her up, carried her across, set her down and continued on his way. The rest of the next day, the first monk brooded about the fact that his companion had violated the monastic rules. Finally he could stand it no longer. "How could you touch that woman?" he said to his companion. His companion replied, "Are you still carrying that woman? I set her down by the riverbank."

The second monk, represents the Mahayana path. The deal is for the devotee to be in the world but not of it. It is the activity of mind that is of primary importance, not that of the body. But according to the mainstream of Mahayana thought, the body too is but a form of mind.

This view is really implicit in early Buddhism, but it was not yet clearly formulated. Early Buddhism, after all, recognized that the mind creates the forms of *samsara*. Atoms and sense impressions act on the body through the senses. The body unifies these sensuous messages so that one will judge that the thing one sees as a cat is the same thing one touches and finds soft and hears 'meow.' This unified sense impression is presented to the intellect which puts it in the category of cat and animal in general. This is how the concept of cat is formed, and how all concepts are formed. Thus what the mind knows is relative to the way human beings think. This is already in the *Abhidharma Pitaka*, the first systematic Buddhist philosophy.

So where is the objective, non-mental building block that divides objective reality from the relativistic interpretation of mind? It is nowhere to be found. Later Buddhism was in some views, idealist. But since mind itself is a relativistic concept, and since material reality as we know it is also a mental construct, objective reality cannot be conceptually known or spoken of at all. This does not mean it is not real. And, as we will see later, reality can be known non-conceptually through the activity of meditation.

Because it is so thoroughly non-dualistic, later Buddhism is just as concerned with activity and compassion as with study and wisdom. The Vajrayana thinkers of India and Tibet saw the world not as a static reality to be rejected, but as transformable as the mind itself. Reality is already pure, but it is mistakenly seen as full of suffering and evil. The very activity of meditation removes the obstacles to pure perception and enables the primal purity to shine through.

Vajrayana thinkers see the three paths of Buddhism in the following way: Theravada sees the world as a poison to be rejected; the Mahayana sees it as a poison to be drunk because the antidote of meditation is there; the Vajrayana transforms the poison into nectar.

There is a fairy tale by Hans Christian Anderson called, "The Snow Queen," in which a devil drops and breaks a mirror which horribly distorts anything it reflects. A small splinter enters the heart of a child who then sees the world as evil and vicious. Vajrayana Buddhists see sentient beings as sharing the plight of this child. The *dharma* is designed to remove the splinter of glass so that existence can be recognized as pure from the beginning.

The Development of Mahayana

There is a story about a Tibetan lama who described a certain cave as haunted by evil spirits. When a westerner objected to the tale, dismissing it as a myth, the lama replied, "Do not worry, you are an American. You wouldn't see any demons." Predispositions to see things in certain ways are not always the same.

It might be argued that if experience were so subjective, then all desires would be fulfilled. We need only want things for them to come into existence. The counter argument was only to become clear much later in Buddhist thinking. It is two fold: 1) some things are too deeply imbedded in human history and culture to be mentally cast out, at least by most people; 2) minds are not pure, so they will create monsters and evils, even when we consciously do not want them. Consider the nightmare. We are surprised, frightened, helpless. But we create nightmares with our own minds.

Buddhists do not deny the existence of these gods, demons, etc., which were so much a part of the thinking of their time. Today, too, they would not usually deny the existence of Christ or the Judaeo—Christian God in general. They do deny, however, the existence of a creator god. Mahayanists strove to liberate all and not pass into nirvana until all are saved. Mahayana thinkers argued that since all concepts are artificially imposed on reality by the mind, reality is beyond conception. This includes space and time. The self too, is a mental construction, as well as the distinction between self and others conceived of as separate entities. So if the distinction between self and other is artificial, the liberation of each is connected with the liberation of all.

The good karma created by the bodhisattva in seeking the liberation of all and the intention of the bodhisattva to be reborn for the sake of others, is manifested in the phenomenal world as the reappearance of a person or type of person. So strong are the factors connected with this karma, that the "new" person will have the good intentions of the former incarnation, and even some of his or her "memories." The more perfect the bodhisattva, the closer and more continuous the connections with the past.

Early Mahayana literature concerned itself with the life of the

Buddha (*Lalitavistara*) the *dharma* (*Lotus of the Good Law*) and the miracles of bodhisattvas like Avalokistesvara. These *sutras* were said to be of miraculous origin, according to Tibetan historians such as Buston and Taranatha. But beliefs in bodhisattvas, miracles etc. must be viewed in the context of the *prajnaparamita* literature.

The central idea of the *prajnaparamita* (highest wisdom) literature is the emptiness of all phenomena. This is sometimes mistakenly interpreted as the idea that all is nothing. But emptiness is not nothing; it is reality beyond conception.

This idea was already implied in the Abhidharma, which pinpointed mind as the creator of ordinary knowledge. It is true that the Abhidharma accepted the reality of the world. But what was this reality? There were endless debates. If atoms were real apart from experience, then how could we know them if all our perceptual knowledge is relative to human experience? If they are merely the smallest elements of objects of experience, how could they be different from our ordinary knowledge of the world, which, for example, is experienced as having color. Atoms are thought to be without color.

On the other hand if sense impressions are the basic units of experience (more basic than atoms since atoms are a construction out of them) then they too are functions of mind, not of matter.

The *prajnaparami*ta literature did not deny reality per se. It just denied the reality of anything one might claim was real, because that anything had to be a concept, a mental creation. One could not even say reality was mental for 'mind' and mental' are themselves concepts.

An apparent paradox immediately arises. The *prajnaparamita* literature is said to be the word of the Buddha. But if what the *prajnaparamita* literature says is true, then it cannot really be true because there is no truth that can be expressed in words. Mahayana thinkers in this tradition embraced this paradox, claiming that in actual fact the Buddha never said a single word.

Nagarjuna's Arguments

The ideas of the *Prajnaparamita Sutra* are expressed poetically. But Mahayana philosophers, well trained in Indian logic, expressed them in the form of tightly argued syllogisms. As mentioned before, one of the first of these great Mahayana thinkers was Nagarjuna. Not only did Nagarjuna argue against the reality of the world as perceived by us, but also against the reality of causality, and thus of time. One of his arguments is particularly dramatic. If time is real, there must be a smallest unit, the instant. But only one instant can exist at a time. This, by definition, is the present. But according to our concept of casualty, cause must precede effect. If this is so, if the cause is present, it cannot reach across its moment of time to bring about the effect which must come later. In other words, in an instant without extension there is no time for causal processes to take place. Thus the way we have set up our concept of causality, on analysis, turns out to be an impossible, incoherent description.

But if we redefine reality so that the effect is not separate from the cause, but part of it, the situation is just as bad. If effect D is contained in its cause C, then C, considered as the effect of B, must be contained in B, and B in A and so on. But then all effects must be contained in a single cause. If this is the case there is no longer an explanation for why things happen one event at a time. The very notion of time as the measure of change, so essential to causal thinking, would become incoherent. Further, Nagarjuna points out, if cause and effect were the same, when one ate food one would also be eating excrement.

One might well ask whether or not Nagarjuna's argument would support notions of time as conceived of in modern theoretical physics. But modern physics is itself not very clear on the nature of time. One might guess that it would be consistent with Nagarjuna's views, though not identical with them. Physicists claim that space and time are relative to the point of view of the observer. There is no absolute time or space. And thus if causal relations are classically conceived in terms of cause preceding effect, causality too can only be true relative to the observer.

The conclusions are the same but the ideas are somewhat different. Nagarjuna's arguments are logical rather than empirical. For the physicist, the viewpoint of the observer is inescapable. But for Nagarjuna, a good Buddhist, if the notion of the individual observer is itself incoherent, a result of ignorance, then the lifting of the obscurities due to ignorance should lead to a transcendence of the relative point of view. It is this final insight which saves Nagarjuna from nihilism, from insurmountable skepticism. As the bonds of ignorance fall away from the mind, relative knowledge is left behind and one comes closer and closer to the absolute.

This brings us back to the question raised earlier about nirvana in the early Buddhist tradition. If one extinguishes all desire, why isn't one left merely with a painless state? Why does one experience bliss and perfect fulfillment? The same question in a slightly different form can be raised in connection with Nagarjuna's ideas. If one dissolves the conceptions one has about ordinary life, why isn't one left with absolutely nothing?

The answer involves an aspect of Buddhism that makes it a religion rather than just a philosophy. There is something about reality that is close to our experience of a compassionate, wise, and blissful person. It is not, however, as if the enlightened being were experiencing a different thing than ordinary beings. He or she is experiencing the same reality in a purified way. This is the meaning of 'nirvana is samsara.'

Nirvana is Samsara

A similar problem in philosophy of art may be helpful here. Suppose someone has no appreciation of modern art. For example, consider a father who wants his son to go out and work to make money for the family instead of going to art school. He sees a copy of a drip painting by Jackson Pollack in his son's book. He is enraged that his son is wasting his time on studying what he sees as gobs of ink on canvas.

Then one rainy day, father and son are having a warm and friendly conversation at home. The large living room window is covered with raindrops. As the rain ends, the sun comes out and turns the raindrops into a rainbow of color. The father notices the beauty of this. His son says, "That is the point of the Pollack painting." The father, understanding the value of the interplay of color and form, "sees the picture"; His perception of modern art has been purified and transformed. It is not that he is looking at a different thing when he sees the Pollack painting. He looks at the same thing, but his perception is now aesthetic rather than purely physical. This analogy is helpful in many ways and we will return to it.

Similarly, when a person achieves a high degree of realization, he or she perceives the same reality, but transformed. There is an important point at which, however, the analogy fails. In the example of the painting, there is a material object that can be viewed from a physical point of view (oil paint on canvas) or an aesthetic point of view (beautiful). But in the case of Nagarjuna's absolute level, "thing" is itself a concept which must be discarded.

Nevertheless, the analogy holds in another way. Even though the aesthetically sensitive person's appreciation of a work of art is through his or her mind and seems (and thus is in this sense) subjective it is an objective fact that certain objects lend themselves more readily than others to be perceived as beautiful. Botticelli's "La Primavera," for example, is more readily perceived as beautiful than yesterday's discarded banana peel. Those who fail to see the beauty of this painting might appropriately be called "aspect blind." Perhaps something is keeping them from enjoying the painting. Maybe, for example, they hate anything that involves pagan themes.

Mahayana Buddhists are in effect saying that the enlightened person is to the unenlightened as the aesthetically sensitive person is to one that has no enjoyment of beauty. It is not that they are experiencing a different reality but the same one in a different way. And just as it is an objective fact that "La Primavera" lends itself to being perceived as beautiful by the aesthetically sensitive, so the Buddhists in the later tradition claim it is an objective fact about reality as a whole that it lends itself to being experienced in a special way by the religiously sensitive.

Nagarjuna made explicit the distinction between the absolute and relative level contained in the *prajnaparamita* literature. But although his work is not at all nihilistic, it disturbed many Buddhists who worried that if the Buddha's words do not contain a literal description of reality, then they are useless. And this would seem to be the case if Nagarjuna is right that reality is not describable in any words whatsoever.

There is, however, a solution to this problem. It was worked out slowly in many stages. An important step towards the understanding of this connection was taken by Asanga and his brother Vasubandhu representing two distinct idealist trends in Buddhist thought. Both were intrigued by the ability of the mind to know the world. The mind comes to know primarily through sensation, visual and other; which could be called external sensations. Given the type of mind, human, animal, etc., these sensations are organized in various ways. And humans then reason about these organized sensations and produce a conceptual system.

Idealism

Asanga and Vasubandhu, two fourth-century Buddhists, accepted the view that there has to be both a knower and an object of knowledge. But is the knower one or many? Are the objects one or many? And are the objects and the knower metaphysically (really) different as well as epistemologically (believed to be) different?

Asanga, admitting that we only know reality through habitual patterns, concludes that this is true of the mind as well. The categories of experience that include number, object, etc. cannot be applied in a non -relativistic manner to that which knows. Mind, therefore, cannot be claimed in any absolute sense to be one or many, subject or object, material vs. immaterial, etc. Asanga then, falls short of claiming that mind alone exists. But neither is mind simply a subjective entity that can be contrasted on the relative level with another non-mental reality. This is because self and other are categories which the mind imposes on things. These distinctions are not part of the world. All distinctions arise from mind, but the distinctions themselves are not part of the original flow of consciousness. Consciousness is like a river which we divide into two tributaries of subject and object. Strictly speaking, it is not even correct to call this river "mind." It is simply the system of causality, of inter-dependent co origination. By analogy, when one sees a mirage of water in the road, this is a trick played on the mind. Yet it occurs because of the causal interaction between the optical nerve, brain, light, road surface, etc. Similarly, experience is a result of the interplay of causal conditions which results in the "mirage" of subject and object.

Modern analytic philosophers such as G. E. Moore criticized idealists for views like this, claiming that if, for example, time were unreal, then we would have no right to talk about someone being early for an appointment. But Buddhists such as Asanga would argue that on the level of the mirage (relative level) there are distinctions to be made such as "early" and "late." One is only in error when one tries to conceive of these concepts non-relativistically. Early and late, hot and cold, etc. all derive their meaning from a web of interconnected concepts on the relative level. On this level they are perfectly valid. Nor is it surprising that this "walking with a stick"(or skillful means) is so successful. Myself as subject and the object, the cat, are both spun by the same web of interdependent causes.

Let's return to the question of the validity of Buddhist scriptures. The analogy with aesthetic experience is again useful. There are certain non-aesthetic experiences which may be said to be particularly helpful in acquiring an aesthetic sense. The feel of soft sand, the sound of the sea, the warmth of the sun, while not in themselves aesthetic are likely to lead to an aesthetic experience. Similarly, the words of the Buddha are of such a nature (although themselves not absolute) as to lead to an experience of the true nature. This is their function in the system of inter-dependent co-origination, i.e., cause and effect.

Of course, no one could know for sure that the Buddhist path does lead to an experience of the true nature without actually having this experience. Similarly, one cannot know for sure that anyone can have an experience of beauty unless one experiences beauty for oneself. All philosophy can do is to show that various perspectives on reality are possible. The proof that a given perspective may be taken must remain a matter of personal discovery. Otherwise, the result of non-conceptual meditation aimed at transcending relativistic concepts could not be distinguished from a dreamless sleep or simple self extinction. The enlightenment state is filled with qualities which elude description, because our linguistic categories are meaningful only on the level of ordinary points of view.

The experience of emptiness, or the true nature, athough transcending attempts to describe it, is similar to perfect unending happiness, without suffering or difficulty of any kind. Just as physical happiness, aesthetic happiness , psychological happiness and moral happiness, though different, are not totally dissimilar to one another, so the happiness of enlightenment bears some similarity to happiness on the other levels.

But if this is the true nature, and all the miseries of our world result from distorted, incomplete perceptions, how did these inadequacies arise in the first place? After all, they do not exist apart from the true nature.

The answer to this question was provided in Buddhism in terms of two concepts, that of the six poisons affecting the mind (anger, hatred, jealousy and attachment, ignorance and fear), and the related idea of the *alaya* or storehouse consciousness. As mentioned earlier, it is craving and ignorance which produce the idea that reality is made of material objects and that we are material beings. The six poisons reinforce these ideas even more strongly. Starting at birth, we have the tendency to perceive the world and ourselves in material, spatial and temporal terms. Why is this the case? Past karma determines a lot of the way we begin to see the world. Buddhist thinkers would have understood genetic inheritance, particularly of personality, in karmic terms. But even reincarnated saints see the world materially, unless they are at the very highest levels.

All sentient beings share a common unconscious mind, called the *alaya* or storehouse consciousness. This is somewhat similar to Jung's collective unconscious. These unconscious conceptions about the nature of things are so deeply imbedded in the mind that it takes a fully enlightened being to see through them and in doing so, to gain some control over the karmic forces affecting himself or herself and other people. Mipham Rinpoche in his commentary on the *Madhyamakalankara* describes the *alaya* in the following way: "The term all-ground consciousness (the *alaya*), is applied to [that aspect of] one's consciousness that, as mere aware clarity, is not confined to any of the engaged cognitions, but rather which functions as the support for habitual tendencies. It is neutral in essence, a mere awareness of the actuality of objects, and arises momentarily." (Doctor, 2004.p.355. Mipham's commentary to *sloka* 44)

Ordinary bodhisattvas can transform their conscious minds into a pure perception of experience by means of certain mental exercises which we will discuss later. They can even help others to do this. And with the help of perfectly enlightened beings they can affect the *alaya*.

There exist two forms of the *alaya*, pure and impure. The impure *alaya* consciousness is that which is inherited by sentient beings through the workings of karma, in particular as the result of the six poisons. The pure *alaya* is the original perfect state of mind, unaffected by these poisons. With the pure *alaya*, subconscious nightmares are dispelled and replaced by images of beauty, peace and wisdom.

Thus Buddhist Mahayana idealism, called the Chittamatra or "mind only" school provides the answer to a central problem of idealism. Experience is mental, yet resists change, because of the alaya consciousness.

This may seem less strange if one reflects on the nature of dreams. No one would deny that, in a nightmare, it is one's own mind that creates the experience. Yet one can be surprised by terrifying images. Mahayana idealism sees all of experience, when not transformed into pure awareness, as one huge nightmare. If one could imagine transforming and controlling one's own nightmares, one could imagine the task of the Buddhist practitioner in transforming all of his or her waking and sleeping experience. The difference is, of course, that the bodhisattva considers the nightmares of all beings as his or her own and will not rest until the experience of all sentient beings is transformed.

Asanga, agreeing with Nagarjuna that the nature of all things is emptiness, attempts to explain the way in which emptiness manifests itself. It manifests itself as mind, pure at first. But because of the six poisons(anger, hatred, jealousy, craving, ignorance, fear), experience has become corrupt and degenerate. (There is a disagreement among scholars on whether or not Asanga and Vasubandhu thought of the mind as absolutely real, or rather, thought that its nature is emptiness. It seems clear, however, that the Chittamatra thinkers against whom Shantarakshita is arguing thought of the mind as having ultimate existence.)

But now the question remains as to why the six poisons should ever have come about from the perfect manifestation of emptiness. The answer is subtle and paradoxical and really only becomes clear later in the Vajrayana tradition in which the poisons themselves are seen in a transformed way as wisdoms.

Yet the answer is also already implicit in the Madhyamaka school of Nagarjuna and the Chittamatra school of Asanga. If the nature of reality is emptiness, then since emptiness is perfect, all beings are already perfectly enlightened although they do not realize it. This idea is understood at least to some extent in the following way. Through the operation of karma, all beings are led throughout their various lifetimes to an understanding of the true nature. All eventually will reach enlightenment. But since time, space and number are applicable only on the relative level, on the absolute level enlightenment already exists. Thus to the enlightened mind all evil, illusion, etc. are seen as not existing on the absolute level.

This has exposed late Buddhist thought to the criticism that the Buddhist practitioner would see, for example, Hitler as good, and approve the genocide of the Jews. The answer to this objection necessitates an understanding of the way in which concepts operate on different perspectival levels. First it is necessary to distinguish between indigenous predicates and borrowed predicates.
A predicate is indigenous within a perspective if it acquires its original meaning from that perspective. For example, on the physical object level, heavy, balanced, fat, etc. are indigenous predicates. A predicate is borrowed if its original meaning is derived from one perspective, but is used in a new way on another. For example,

balance in art is borrowed from physics. It has a new meaning, however. This is shown from the fact that, if we say of a picture that it is nicely 'balanced' we would not place it on the sill of an open window on the grounds that because it is balanced it will not fall down. Further, someone who lacked the aesthetic perspective might not be at all clear about what we meant when we said the painting was balanced.

"Rotten" is a physical indigenous predicate. If we say an action is rotten, this is borrowed. We do not try to cut out the rottenness from the action the way we would cut it out of a peach. "Cruelty" is indigenous to the moral perspective. We punish cruel people but not cruel paintings.

Similarly, when we say "reality is good" on the level of the religious perspective, we do not mean the same thing as on the moral perspective. A good person on the moral level will struggle unrelentingly against cruelty. Not so on the absolute level. There is no point to punishment on this level any more than there would be to punishing a painting of Hitler. Thus an unenlightened person cannot even know clearly what it means to say "reality is wisdom."

There is some connection, however, between the meaning of borrowed predicates and their indigenous use. That is why they are so apt. The connection is in experience. There is some similarity for example between our experience of balance in a painting and our experience of balance in nature. It is, however, impossible to state exactly what this is. It is somehow intuited. So there's also some similarity between our experience of a wise person and reality as wisdom.

Does this mean that reality is like a person, a kind of God? After all, some Buddhists do visualize the universe as Buddha and each atom as Buddha? But, strictly speaking, one cannot say that the true nature either has or has not personal qualities. Such categories cannot apply. Yet there are meditation techniques which direct one to visualize the universe as the body of Buddha, all sounds as the voice of Buddha, and all thoughts as the thoughts of Buddha. There is no doubt that this person like imagery is very forceful. It instills devotion, which encourages effort, patience, courage, strength. Yet, ultimately, it is only skillful means, pointing to what is nameless. There is, therefore, no contradiction between the religious assertion that reality is wise, perfect, good, etc. and the moral assertion that evil exists and we must do all we can to eliminate it. One must not confuse the perspectives. To do so would be like someone saying, "This painting has a charming lightness, so I can throw it in the lake and it won't sink." Rather, one's very appreciation of the lightness of the painting will make one take care that it never falls into the water. One's appreciation of the ultimate will, therefore, inspire one to take care of all the other levels. The more complex levels of experience enrich the simpler ones, the religious enriching the moral and aesthetic, and these in turn enriching physical perceptions. On the absolute level the bodhisattva would see all things as perfect, yet on the relative level, spontaneously act to eliminate all of Hitler's evil ways and deeds. This explains the Buddhist injunction to have a view as vast as the sky and moral conduct as fine as a grain of sand.

Now to return to the question of the truth of the scriptures. The scriptures are said to have come from the Buddha. Probably some of them were spoken by the historical Buddha. But this is not essential. They, like the historical Buddha himself, are a pure manifestation of emptiness. It is, by analogy, as if one were having a nightmare and suddenly a rescuing figure or magic words were to appear in the dream and dispel the evil. The saving power could make use of the fiction of the dream itself to bring about relief from suffering. In other words, the scriptures or the word of the Buddha do not have to be true in an absolutely literal sense. They have pragmatic truth. They are true if they lead beings to enlightenment, and false if they do not. To put it in Wittgenstein's terms, you use philosophy as a ladder. When you have reached your goal, you throw it away. That is why all the refuge prayers state that one will go for refuge to the Buddha, the Dharma, and the Sangha only until enlightenment is reached.

This point was made in another way by Nagarjuna's follower Chandrakirti. According to Chandrakirti, we can know through words, and these words are ultimately without any meaning. Yet because philosophically we can prove their meaninglessness, by this very fact we will become less attached to the world of experience and go directly for the pure consciousness achieved through meditation. The very inadequacy of words shows the way to truth. And the scriptures, such as the *prajnaparamita* literature, which specifically state the limits of words, are of special value.

If on the relative level an idealist conception of reality is generally correct, it is not surprising that Mahayana Buddhists would expect pure and perfect elements of existence to become manifest through the transforming mental power of the buddhas and bodhisattvas. Some of these elements exist within nature such as the lotus flower which is perfectly pure, yet grows within the mud. It is a living lesson that one can transcend the daily horrors of human experience. This same alertness to the lessons of nature existed in the medieval west. One finds it in the symbolism in works of art in this period. The pelican, for example, appears in many paintings because the mother pelican will give her own body to feed her young. The pelican thus becomes a symbol of Christ. The medieval mystic thus perceived lessons in many aspects of nature, such as the purifying effect of water, or the power of light to guide in the darkness. In Islamic Sufism, wine becomes a symbol of the intoxicating joy experienced in union with God. Similarly, mindfulness in Mahayana Buddhism extended to an awareness of the teaching power of all things, and thus their sacredness. The Mahayana evolved from the Theravada (Hinayana) in a logical and inevitable way. From the early view that all is impermanent and that concepts are mental fictions came the conclusions that 1) nothing has a fixed nature and hence everything can always be changed and 2) since the mind creates the reality of samsara, the mind related truth of samsara can be controlled by mental disciplines and techniques. To know the emptiness of this is wisdom; to control one's reactions to things and help others to do so is compassion.

Many clearly realized, however, that this development involved difficulties. It was easy to fall into the extremes of nihilism or eternalism. Nihilism was a danger because philosophies such as Nagarjuna's Madhyamaka tempted some people to believe that, because all conceptual truth was relative truth, everything was unreal and thus liberation from samsara unnecessary. On the other hand, the use of techniques such as images of deities, mantras, etc. could tempt people to think that these divine beings, such as the goddess Tara, had eternal objective reality. (Most religions believe their deities, etc. have this sort of absolute unchanging ontological status and are thus called eternalist by Mahayana Buddhists.)

Clear warnings were given about these extremes, but they were not always heeded. Mahayana teachers, however, believed that the results were well worth the risks, for in this way many could reach liberation who otherwise would not have had this opportunity.

Vajrayana

Madhyamaka metaphysics reinforced and explained the doctrine of impermanence. If nothing has a fixed nature, if there are in reality no substances, then that explains why things can change. Further, if all we know is constructed by knowledge based on sensation, and evil is a result of the way in which this process operates (because of the six poisons; hatred, anger, greed, jealousy, fear, ignorance), then we can construct a pure relative truth through the senses by eliminating these poisons. It follows that nothing in our experience need be avoided. Rather, the way in which we experience must be transformed. One helpful image suggested by Huston Smith, in the film "Requiem for a Faith," is that of the ocean which to a drowning person is terrifying, but brings great pleasure to an experienced swimmer. To learn to swim correctly, an experienced teacher is essential. And the techniques for transforming experience must also be taught by a "realized" person who not only can experience the world as pure but can also understand and remember the way ordinary unrealized people perceive.

These techniques are the heart of the Vajrayana, the lineage of Shantarakshita. While being very similar to Mahayana, it differs with respect to one's attitude towards the world. Mahayana practices and meditation are designed as an antidote to poisons in the world in which the practitioner lives. Vajrayana techniques are designed to transform these poisons.

One cannot, of course, describe anything in terms of the absolute level. It is beyond conception. It would have to be, because by definition the absolute level is transcendent to any particular point of view. It is said to be experienced by enlightened beings, but apart from their expressions of bliss, compassion and wisdom, this level is unknown to us. The absolute is, however, described as being like a crystal which throws out many different lights, which are the manifestations of the relative level

The Vajrayana emphasizes the mental space which is visualized as the palace of the deity, often complete with towers, rooms and gardens. All smells and tastes are seen as the perfumes and nectars of the deity. For example, a person living within such a mandala might seem to an outsider to be drinking a glass of water or wine. From the point of view of the practitioner, he or she is drinking the nectar of the gods from a jeweled cup. The experience of the practitioner has become perfectly beautiful and pure. Finally the deity is pictured as dissolving into light and entering the heart of the visualizer. All distinction between object and visualizer disappears and the practitioner experiences himself or herself as the deity. Eventually the deity is itself recognized in its true nature as emptiness. The visualization is dissolved and the practitioner remains in non-conceptual meditation. Finally the practitioner returns to the ordinary world thinking that he or she has done the meditation in order to transform the world of samsara into a pure buddhafield for all beings. Here we come to the solution to the problem mentioned earlier about the nature of nirvana. Early Buddhism provided no clear answer to the question about why non-attachment should produce an experience of beauty, perfection and bliss rather than simply a dull absence of pain. In the Vajrayana one comes to understand that this bliss results from the nature of reality. Although beyond conception, reality seems to the practitioner to be of such a nature as to lend itself to being experienced in such a way as to give rise to wisdom, compassion, power and bliss. These are the qualities perceived from the perspective of enlightenment. The image of the god and goddess in union therefore is clearly a most appropriate metaphor for being itself. And since we are part of reality, the ability to experience that bliss is within our own nature.

Notes:
Burtt, E.A. *The Teachings of the Compassionate Buddha* New York: Mentor, 1981
Dongyal, Khenpo Tsewang: *Floweres of Expanding Joy*, Sarnath, Pema Samye Chokhor Ling, 1999
Doctor, Thomas *Speech of Delight: Mipham's Commentary on Santaraksita's Ornament of the Middle Way* Ithaca: Snow Lion
Nagarjuna *Mulamadhyamakakarika (The Fundamental Wisdom of the Middle Way)* trans. And commentary by Garfield, Jay L. Oxford: Oxford university press, 1995

CHAPTER 2

THE INTRODUCTION OF BUDDHISM INTO TIBET

Pre-Buddhist Beliefs

Tibet's role in recorded history does not predate the seventh century. It was at this time that it became a unified kingdom. The center of this kingdom was the Yarlung Valley. Lhasa, a hunting reserve, was fifty-five miles southwest.

The first Yarlung kings were said to be descended from heaven and at the end of their lives returned to heaven by means of a sacred cord. The early kings were considered to be godlike beings. Although the heavenly cord was said to be severed by one of these kings, an air of sacredness continued to surround their earth bound successors.

Because Bonpo beliefs had such a strong hold on the minds of the Tibetans, when the Buddhist teachers came to Tibet, they sometimes used Bonpo names, as Buddha used Hindu words in a new way, when he first taught the dharma in India, so that the words would be understandable to the people. Similarly, Khenchen Shantarakshita, Guru Padmasambhava and the other pandits and translators used Tibetan words that were familiar to the native population. They never used language the people could not understand. So they kept the ancient Tibetan terminology and used it to explain the Dharma.

The central role of Madhyamaka concepts in Tibetan Buddhism clearly distinguishes this religion from all native beliefs. Whatever the native religion was and whatever its origin it had no sophisticated metaphysics on the level of Indian thought. For such a tradition one needs a literary and scholarly base, impossible in an illiterate population.

Nargarjuna's logic, in conjunction with an idealist view of relative truth, necessitated a middle ground between externalism and nihilism. That is, since on analysis, the world in itself must be understood as transcending our subjective concepts of it, we cannot say any of the objects of religious worship are absolutely real. Since on the relative level all our concepts are created by mind, custom and habit will dictate what will seem real to us. Thus on the relative level, there was no contradiction in the Buddhist use of native Tibetan concepts once they had been transformed into Buddhist terms. This is 'skillful means'. Yet unlike the native religion, nor like even the most sophisticated forms of Hinduism, the Buddhists never accepted deities as either creators or eternally real. They are part of the ebb and flow of mind.

It is, of course, easy to try to see Tibetan Buddhism as a synthesis of Indian Buddhism and native Tibetan religion. But this would be a big mistake. It would be like seeing European Christianity as an equal mixture of barbaric religion and Hellenistic Christianity. For example, one could argue, if one took this view, that since some barbarians practiced human sacrifice, the Christian mass was a more humane version of this. But that would be to ignore the fact that the Christian mass predated the influx of Christianity into barbarian Europe. Some barbarian converts may have seen the mass as a form of human sacrifice because they were used to thinking in these terms. And missionaries may not have stressed the difference, because they were eager to make contact with the people. Traditional holidays and ritual objects such as solstices and mistletoe were incorporated for similar reasons. But it would be a mistake for such reasons to identify Christian practices with those of the Druids.

Actually, the most reasonable view of the introduction of Buddhism to Tibet is that of a mighty Indian seed that fell on fertile Tibetan soil, producing a strong, healthy plant.

Vajrayana practices were made more acceptable to the Tibetan people by casting concepts into native Tibetan terminology. The Indian dharmapalas (dharma protectors), for example, upon joining the Tibetan pantheon, were given Tibetan names. Dharmapalas of Tibetan origin, were also added to the Indian pantheon. Part of the temptation to consider Tibetan Buddhism as part Bonpo is probably due to the fact that in the case of the importing of tantra into Tibet, the hand fit the glove so well. Tantric practice in India was really not well suited to the culture. The caste system and Brahmin conceptions of the appropriate and the hygienic made the tantric lack of distinction in these matters anathema. If a high caste yogi was discovered to have taken a low caste girl for his consort, there was a terrible scandal. Tibetan culture, however, was more democratic and open. The people were earthy and high spirited and in general saw no harm in the tantra. They were used to seeing deities in many special places, so visualization came easily to them. Whatever resistance they had to Buddhism consisted mainly in a dislike of its foreignness and a fear that adherence to it would offend the local deities.

The Birth of Philosophy in Tibet: Historical Background

By the seventh century, there were already many monks in Tibet, mostly from Central Asia. But India was regarded as the purest source of Buddhist teachings. It was, after all, the native land of Buddha Sakyamuni. And it had a network of monasteries and universities which were the depositories of more than a thousand years of Buddhist studies. So, in the eighth century, King Thri Srong Detsen sent his emissary Ba Salnang (*gBa gsalsnang*) to search for the sage best able to introduce Buddhist philosophy to the Tibetan people. The people were illiterate. Their temperament was warlike. Their religion centered on divination and animal sacrifice. The emissary met Shantarashita, then professor of philosophy and abbot of Nalanda University, and invited him to Tibet.

Nalanda was an enormous university containing more than two thousand faculty members in many different schools of medicine, humanities, arts and sciences. The Indian people had inherited a tradition of learning already more than fifteen hundred years old. Their books were recorded in the sacred Sanskrit language. Although Buddhist philosophy predominated at this time, scholars debated freely with proponents of a dozen other traditions. There were, as well, many sects of Buddhism rivaling each other in their standards of clarity, precision and persuasiveness.

Shantarakshita agreed to leave Nalanda university and come to Tibet. In the brief period before his death he established the Indian Buddhist tradition, built a network of monastic colleges and trained a generation of philosophers and teachers. In a few years, Tibet was a citadel of Buddhist learning.

Shantarakshita was literally a treasury of all that had gone before in Indian thought. He not only knew the formidable canon of Buddhist philosophy, but had mastered Hindu, Jain and Carvaka philosophy as well. His great work, the *Tattvasamgraha (The Compendium of Truth)*, including the commentary of his student Kamalashila, is a defense of Mahayana Buddhism against the arguments of other schools. It is one of the most comprehensive and subtle philosophical treaties ever written. (Since their views are basically in accord, I will not distinguish these philosophers in this study.

The *Madhyamakalankara (The Ornament of the Middle Way)* is less comprehensive. In it Shantarakshita criticizes those views which he believes deserve the most serious philosophical consideration. His most important contribution in this work is his careful analysis of the complex forms of the idealist view and his discussion of their positive as well as negative features. In the *Tattvasiddhi (The Attainment of Suchness)*, Shantarakshita reveals himself as a tantric master, and presents a transcendental argument defending the possibility of tantric realization.

The question of causality is a good example of this type of problem. It is certainly a lively issue today. How can cause be said to precede effect except relatively when time is relative? Do modern scientists really believe that a cause brings about an effect when all that appears is constant conjunction of events, justifying only statistical probability that similar events will occur together in the future? Nevertheless we do exerience temporally. One Tibetan lama, Khenchen Palden Sherab Rinpoche spoke of a "fourth time" which is the source of our experience of past, present and future. It seems to function as a hypothetical construct, pointing to a nonparadoxical temporality beyond conception.

The Tattvasamgraha

In the *Tattvasamgraha*, Shantarakshita argues against all the views (most of which he does not identify by name) contrary to his

Yogacara Svatantrika position. When describing the *Tattvasamgraha*, it is tempting to merely list the various views opposed to Shantarakshita's own, and present his and his student Kamalashila's answers. But this is not helpful, for two reasons. First of all, some of the views he is refuting are not philosophically important today, as, for example, the idea that the world emerged from an eternal seed syllable. Secondly, Shantarakshita, being eager to convince his opponents, is often content to show particular inconsistencies, rather than to present rock bottom philosophical arguments against fundamental principles.

On the other hand, it would be a mistake to present Shantarakshita's views only in the framework of contemporary concerns. For some of the problems he addresses, though neglected by the contemporary philosophical community, are nonetheless important. So I will try to find a middle ground between historical interest and pure analysis.

Shantarakshita's school is known as Yogacara-Madhyamaka. Yeshay Day (*Ye-shes-sde*) (c.800), who translated Shantarakshita's work into Tibetan, explains this in the following way:

"In the Madhyamaka treatises composed by the master, the Superior (Nagarjuna), and his spiritual son (Aryadeva), the mode of existence or non-existence of external objects is not clarified. After that, the master Bhavaviveka refuted the system of the Vijnaptikas (Yogacarins) and posited a system of the conventional existence of external objects. Then the master Shantarakshita, relying on Yogacara texts, constructed a different system of Madhyamaka which taught that external objects do not exist conventionally and that the mind lacks inherent existence ultimately. Thus, the Madhyamakas arose as two types, the former called the *Sautrantika-Madhyamakas* and the latter, the *Yogacara-Madhyamakas*." Ye-shes sde, Differences Between the Views (*lTa ba'i khad par*) Peking 5847 .

Further, Shantarakshita's school is known as Svatantrika (autonomous) Madhyamaka. Svatantrika is a complicated subject. (The early masters such as Shantarakshita and Chandrakirti did not divide themselves into the schools of Svatantrika and Prasangika that arose later in Tibet.)

To explain briefly, hopefully not misleadingly, the Svatantrikas accept the mode of reasoning that uses a logical argument to establish the truth of a conclusion in the mind of an opponent. For example, in Western terms, 'All men are mortal. Socrates is a man. Therefore Socrates is mortal', establishes the truth of the probandum (conclusion) 'Socrates is mortal'. Svatantrikas defend their acceptance of conclusions on the level of relative truth. Another school, the Prasangika, does not agree that the truth of the conclusion is established even conventionally. Although they use syllogisms, their main method of refuting an opponent is to show a contradiction in what that person is saying. Their reason for this is because they believe the conclusions of autonomous syllogisms falsely imply that these conclusions are true. Svatantrikas would say that although our perceptions do not reflect absolute truth, nevertheless, in the form of a syllogism they provide a sign which can lead us out of the jungle of illusion. Although Shantarakshita's view is correctly characterized as Svatantrika, he never sets himself up in opposition to Prasangikas or specifically to Chandrakirti. In fact, these distinctions did not exist during his lifetime.

Shantarakshita and Causality

Let us begin with the subject of causality, which is certainly a lively issue today. How can cause be said to precede effect except relatively when time is relative? Do modern scientists really believe that a cause brings about an effect when all that is available are general laws providing predictability based on past occurrences, which give us, at best, statistical probability?

Shantarakshita's critique of ideas about causality current during his time is derived from Nagarjuna. To reiterate, Nagarjuna had argued that if we assume 1) time exists moment after moment (a moment being an indivisible instant), 2) the cause at time A (the whole set of root cause plus background conditions, i.e., the state of the universe at time A produces the effect at time B, and 3) that time A and time B are separate moments of time, (A preceding B), then it follows that the cause cannot produce the effect because, when the effect is there, the cause is not, and when the cause is, the effect is not. (A similar argument is also used by Descartes in attempting to prove the existence of God. God is needed to recreate oneself at every moment because the cause cannot stay around long enough to bring the effect into existence . Descartes applies this argument not just to the self, but to the entire universe. Descartes, 1983, p. 11)

It is interesting to contrast these two thinkers. Descartes takes the problem of causality, as we have set it up, with total seriousness. Thus he needs a God to "prop up" the causal relationship when it ceases to make sense. Nagarjuna, on the other hand, is content to show that on the absolute level we do not know what we are talking about when we assert causal relationships. They only make sense within the network of human habits and expectations. For Nagarjuna and Shantarakshita neither the idea that time is momentary nor that it is not, make sense on the absolute level.

A lively concern of Shantarakshita's contemporaries was the issue-of whether or not the effect could be explained as already existing in the cause. This was the position of the Samkhyas, a Hindu school which held that all phenomena evolved out of *prakriti* (nature). The Samkhyas argued that since something cannot come from nothing, all things must come from primordial matter. All things pre-existed in their original cause.

Kamalashila argues that it is just as difficult to understand how a uniform primordial matter (*prakriti*) could produce all the varieties of things as to understand how one moment could simply follow another (text 28). And, if all causes and effects come from the same undifferentiated primordial matter, how can they be different from one other? Yet, they must be different, or one could not tell them apart. One could not even know primordial matter was a cause. But if they are really different then they cannot have the same essence. The Samkhyas predictably reply that the effect is a modification of the cause, not a complete change. But, as Kamalashila points out in his commentary, the concept of modification will not get them out of their difficulty. If a modification took place it would either involve a modification of the original "form" or it would not. If the original form were unmodified, one could perceive cause and effect simultaneously, e.g., old age in youth. If the original form were modified, the old form would have disappeared so one could never know whether or not the new form was like the original. Also the modification could not be of the part or of the whole. It cannot be of the part because all comes from primordial matter which has no parts. Nor can it be a modification of the whole because then we would have a new thing and primordial matter would not be eternal.

Samkhyas argue that they do not really mean that the effect actually exists in the cause but only potentially. Shantarakshita's answer has a modern ring (text 20). He rejects the idea that existing potentially is any different from plain nonexisting. This is the classic western argument against the old potentiality-actuality theory of Aristotle. The oak tree, for example, cannot be said to exist even potentially in the acorn, somewhat like a small, leafy ghost. What does Shantarakshita himself mean by potentiality? Probably just that given a root cause (a seed, for example) and the right conditions (rain, soil, etc.) we will observe, after a time, the growing of a plant. This will happen again and again. To adapt David Hume's view a bit out of context, causality is a habit of mind (see (text 72 comm. "Invariant concomitance").

Shantarakshita on the Existence and Nature of God

In chapter II, Shantarakshita discusses the claim that God is the creator of the universe. First he gives the Nyaya argument from design (text 46) that because natural objects have an orderly structure, they, like jars, must have a conscious producer. (This is, of course, the famous teleological argument for the existence of God). It is impossible to do justice here to all the subtleties of the reply. In brief, Shantarakshita argues, when the Nyayaikas claim that the existence of order in a jar is evidence of an intelligent cause, and so the order of the world is evidence of a divine intelligence, they beg the question at issue. Everyone agrees that a perceptible design must have a cause, but this does not entail that the cause must be intelligent. For example, the Nayaikas argue that just as one perceives an arrangement of parts in a temple and infers a builder, then if one perceives an arrangement of parts in bodies, mountains, etc., it is correct to infer a builder. Shantarakshita replies that it is not obvious that bodies or mountains are arranged at all, and even if they were that would not prove that they have an intelligent cause. One would first have to establish 'invariant concomitance" (TS text 61-62) of arrangements with intelligent causes.

Further, God is said to be one, and when we look at the various things on earth that are made we find many different makers (TS text 81). But then we have no reason to assume one god is the creator of all the things in the world (TS text 73). The world is very different from God, who is perfect. So it is wrong to infer that god is the creator of the jar or any other worldly object (TS text 72).

As further argument against God's existence, Shantarakshita argues (TS text 76), that an eternal being cannot produce anything in time because it is outside of time and the changing world. The Nyayaikas argued that there must be a God who is teacher, because there is no other way to account for knowledge. You cannot have an infinite regress of teachers. Shantarakshita has two answers to this: a) (TS text 84) because of reincarnation, consciousness and knowledge are not completely lost (this is Plato's solution in *The Meno*); b) saying that teaching started with a particular person called God does not get you out of the problem of beginningless "dependence on mutual teaching." It would leave the fact of God's knowledge unaccounted for. If one cannot account for knowledge, ultimately, why bring God up at all?

Next Shantarakshita introduces the possibility (held by some theistic Samkhyas, followers of the Yoga system) that the world is caused by God and primordial matter working together, just as a potter uses clay to make a jar (TS text 94). But Shantarakshita points out that the same objections raised earlier would also apply. Since both God and primordial matter are said to be absolutely simple, they cannot interact to produce the variety existing in the world.

The Samkhya theists might reply (TS text 97-100) that God creates by coming into contact with the three aspects of nature, i.e., with brightness, force and matter. Since these three aspects are necessarily consecutive in their function, their creation is produced consecutively, even though God is changeless.

Shantarakshita answers this in the following way. The capacity to perform all creative acts must be with God-/Primordial Matter in an absolutely timeless way since both are simple and unchanging. But if this is the case, there is nothing to prevent all their creative activity from occurring simultaneously. Indeed it must (TS text 101-102) because since they are changeless, no particular potency can disappear to reappear later (texts 104-105).

Finally Shantarakshita attacks the position of those who declare that the Spirit ('*Purusha*', meant as *Ishvara* - the Lord) created all things. His arguments are similar to those raised against the Nyayaika. Most of the same arguments which apply to God apply to the world spirit. The main difference between the term Purusha and the term God is that they have slightly different connotations. God is said to be the efficient cause of the world, whereas the Purusha is both the efficient and constituent cause, i.e., the world is said to have the nature of *Purusha*. The new arguments of this chapter mainly have to do with the issue of compassion. If the *Purusha* created the world, being all-good, it would never allow suffering. It would create only happy, good beings and never allow them to perish. But suffering and death exist, so there can be no *Purusha*, as Hume was to argue a millennium later.

There is one curious argument (TS text 161). Shantarakshita considers the possibility that the Purusha created the world not out of mercy and compassion, but rather, was motivated by the desire for amusement. But this, Shantarakshita argues, would make the *Purusha* dependent on "the implements of amusement" that is, "creation, sustenance and dissolution of the world", etc. (commentary). The second argument is the variation of those in chapters II and III. If the *Purusha* is all powerful, it would bring about simultaneously all the things which would amuse it.

Shantarakshita and the nature of the self

In chapter VII, Shantarakshita begins his analysis of the nature of the self. It is a different concept from that of the *Purusha*, which is consciousness per se. The self is the one (person?) that has consciousness (TS text 171-176). His criticism in this chapter is mainly directed against arguments claiming that since all that is known is the result of a process of knowing, there must be a distinction between a substantial knower and what is known. Shantarakshita again reminds us   such a distinction involves an infinite regress (TS text 190 commentary). For if the knower is a substantial self who also has self-knowledge, then there must be a knower that knows the knower, etc., ad infinitum, which is absurd.

Shantarakshita accepts the argument that the existence of a cognizer is indubitable because it would be self -contradictory to doubt that there was a doubter. But in relation to the Cartesian question and answer "How often am I? As often as I think," unlike Descartes, he sees no reason to believe that the cognizer is the same in every cognition. It changes as the cognition changes. It is inseparably bound up with the cognition in the momentary conjunction of interdependent conditions. Although called by a single name (self or soul), consciousness is not a single enduring entity. If it were, there would have to be a self that knows the knower each time we think about the knower. Again this leads to an infinite regress of knowers, which is absurd. Cf Kamalashila's commentary to TS text 190 . (To understand the self you have to treat it into an object of knowledge, in which case you have left out the knower. And if you treat that knower as an object of knowledge you get another knower which leads to an infinite regress. And if you want to say all these infinite regressive knowers are reducible to one knower, that one knower cannot be an object of knowledge. So you cannot assert its existence.)

The Nyaya school had argued that the self is necessary to serve as the substratum of desires and enduring selves are causally necessary conditions of desire. Shantarakshita asks (TS text 191-192) what they mean by the cause of desire. He readily admits that desires are caused. But, he says, when the Nyayaikas assert that the self is a sustaining causal condition of desires etc. in the form of a receptacle, they are being misled by an inappropriate picture. Receptacles are only needed with things that will move if not restrained. cf Kamilasila's commentary to TS texts 191-192 . The jujube fruit, for example, is placed in a container, so the pieces won't roll all over. But with desires, perceptions etc. there is no place for them to move to, so they do not need to inhere in anything.

Another important Nyaya argument for the existence of a single self, or cognizer, is that we are able to recall the past through memory and identify such past experiences as our own. Shantarakshita claims that the conclusion, that there is a single cognizer, begs the question. We do not know if we are correctly identifying the subject of the past experience with the present rememberer of it. It is possible that these experiences of perceiving etc. have the peculiar ability to produce the illusion that there is a continuing cognizer.

Shantarakshita then (TS text 197) uses the same form of argument he used in the case of God and primordial matter to argue that an unchanging, eternal self cannot be the cause of phenomena that occur in sequence. If the self as cause is unchanging and eternal, the efficient cause of perceptions, desires etc., being always present, would produce all of them all at once. This of course is not the case, so an unchanging self as cause need not exist.

The Nyayaikas argued that a single cognizer must produce the six cognitions of the senses, e.g., the sight of a dancing girl, the sound of the drum, etc. because they are produced in succession.. But actually, Shantarakshita replies, the eye sees the color, the ear hears the sound etc. all at the same time. These different impressions of the dancing girl do happen all at once, so again, they cannot have a single, enduring unchanging self as cause. (TS texts 200- 201 comm). The Nyayikas also formulated the very simple argument that since we have a single term 'soul' there must be a single entity to which it corresponds. Shantarakshita replies (text 202-206) 1) "existence of synonyms shows there is no unique relationship between word and object e.g. *kava* and *sharira* both mean "body". 2) Words are often used to refer to nonexistent entities, e.g., the sky lotus. The reason this is possible is due to the conventional nature of language. We can use words to mean whatever we like: "Convention proceeds from the independent desire of men (to give a certain name to a certain thing); and terms also are expressive of that alone; wherefore then could there be any restriction of their use?" (TS text 206 commentary). The Nayayaikas also argued that the soul is the cause of breathing and that at death, it is the departure of the soul which causes the cessation of breathing, etc. Shantarakshita replies (TS texts 206-208) that there is no well established connection (invariant concomitance) between soul and breathing. Nor can there be, because soul is an incoherent concept. Just as there can be no invariant concomitance between absence of the son of the barren woman and absence of breathing, so there can be none between absence of the soul and absence of breathing. Further, breathing is sequential, and soul is said to be an unchanging eternal substance. So, soul could not in any case be the cause of such a sequential process. And thus, the absence of breathing at death is not caused by the absence of soul.

One of Shantarakshita's most interesting arguments concerns the Nyayaika claim that the self knows itself. He casts this claim in a Cartesianlike form (TS text 212); "Others have assumed that the 'Soul is proved by Perception; because 'I consciousness' is self-cognizable, and the soul forms the object of that consciousness." Shantarakshita replies (TS texts 212-214) that the soul cannot be the object of the "I" consciousness, because the claim is that the soul is eternal, omnipresent, intelligent, but "not the slightest manifestation of these characters is perceived in 'I' consciousness; the manifestation which is perceived in 'I' consciousness is all in connection with fair complexion and other conditions of the body as is apparent in such expressions as 'I am fair, with weak powers of vision, lean, beset with acute pain' and so forth." (TS texts 213-214 commentary). The soul is clearly not the sort of thing which can be said to be fair complexioned etc. So this "I" consciousness cannot be consciousness of the soul. Shantarakshita's opponents claimed that the notion of the soul is clear. But as Shantarakshita points out there is nothing to be found in "I" consciousness that clearly has the form of soul (TS text 213-214). The commentary to TS text 220 concludes in a very interesting way. Kamalashila admits there is an 'I' consciousness and a mind associated with it. This mind is not part of the body. But like the body, it is momentary. In this sense one could call this momentary mind the soul. But 'soul' does not denote a substance of any kind, much less an eternal substance.

In a modern mode one might call the 'I' the ability to use the first-person pronoun. In a Buddhist context, it would not be just the ability, but also the tendency to do so. It is this tendency, the grasping aspect of existence, which is the root of suffering. "Person", by contrast, functions like "chariot" as a convenient term for a collection of aggregates. Failure to understand this distinction is perhaps the reason that later Buddhist writers accused Shantarakshita of believing the person was real in the sense of an unchanging substance.

Shantarakshita then takes up the claim (chapter VII) that the self is sentience, which for the Mimamsas is the same as cosmic intelligence. This view was held notably by the Mimamsa theologian Kumarila Bhatta, who believed that the self has two kinds of states, "inclusive" and "exclusive". Only inclusive states are permanent.

They include intelligence, substance and being (TS text 222). The exclusive states are those which are experienced in mutually exclusive ways, such as pleasure and pain. The self is like a snake which coils and uncoils. It changes shape but remains always a snake. Its whole character neither disappears completely, nor is there a continuation of its whole character (TS text 223 commentary); "Its states of pleasure, etc., go on disappearing and appearing again, but intelligence permeates all these states; hence there is no incompatibility between the 'exclusive' and 'inclusive' states."

Kumarila's argument for this is as follows (TS text 226). If the soul were to utterly disappear at every moment and a completely new soul were to reappear at every moment, then there would be no way to explain how we identify those actions in the past which we have done; the doer would not be there to come into contact with the effect of the act. But if the self were completely unchanging, then there would be no way it could experience contrary feelings of pain and pleasure.

In TS texts 229-237, Shantarakshita formulates the core of the Mimamsa argument that the Buddhist view of the self cannot account for the temporal aspect of experience. If the object is not different from the knower, than we can never say 'I saw x then, and I see it again now.' If the 'I 'is in the past, we can say the former but not the latter. If in the present, vice versa. The sentence "I saw it in the past" would not be true. We cannot thus speak truly about past and future experiences as a continuum if there is no enduring self. Nor can the self be a series of moments, because a series is not an entity and only an entity can be a knower.
Shantarakshita interrupts his presentation of the Mimamsa argument (Kumarila) at this point to provide us with some useful criticism. The Mimamsa have insisted that intelligence (cognition) is eternal and one. But they also insist that a) cognitions are momentary, and b) cognitions are produced by perception. a) contradicts the principle that cognition is eternal and that cognition has no other nature but intelligence, and b) contradicts the principle that what is eternal cannot be produced.

Shantarakshita then continues with his precis of the Mimamsa argument. The Mimamsas claim that mind is eternal (TS text 242), because it is of the nature of intelligence. The difference in cognitive process (Skt:bodhi,Tib: blo) is due to the diversity of the objects. Shantarakshita has objected that if soul is one and eternal it would know all things simultaneously, rather than consecutively. Kumarila tries to forestall this type of objection (TS text 243) by likening the self to fire which consumes many different things while always remaining fire: "Fire is eternally of the nature of a Burner and yet it does not burn all things at all times. It burns only what is brought to it; and then also, it burns only a thing that is capable of being burnt and not the sky or any other such thing." In the same way a rock crystal mirror stays the same yet reflects whatever is brought in front of it. (TS text 244-245) Cognitive processes similarly reflect only what is presented in a fleeting way by the sense organs, just as the fire only burns what it touches and the mirror only reflects what is brought before it. Thus, the evanescence of cognitive processes are due not to their own nature but because they must reflect truly the nature of what is sensed. And the sense organs perceive in a constantly changing manner. This is the Mimamsa answer to the point that if the self is eternal, it will perceive all things simultaneously. It would indeed do so if it were always in contact with everything, but this is not the case.

In reply, Shantarakshita answers that if cognitive processes are one and eternal, the cognition of sound in a certain case cannot be different from the cognition of taste, etc. But surely this is not true. The cognition of a lemon's taste is very different from the cognition of the sound it makes when it drops. Nor can the analogy with fire be of much help. Because fire too, comes and goes. If it did not, all combustible things would burn all at once. Fire is indeed only a burner when it touches a combustible thing (TS text 256). Thus it is very unlike the eternal, unchanging cognizer. Nor does the analogy with the mirror help the Mimamsa position (TS texts 259-260). Again we are clinging to a false picture. The mirror does not contain the image the way the self as cognizer is said to contain the thought. Nor does the mirror become transformed into the reflection. A glance at the side of the mirror will show it remains the same (TS text 260). If it were really transformed into the reflection, it would be different at every moment, which is just what the Mimamsa do not want to say about the soul. But if the analogy holds and one says that the reflection is illusion, then cognitive processes must be illusory as well.. But how can cognitive processes be illusions when cognition is said to be eternal, unlike illusions which are always transitory (TS text 262)

The arguments contained in the next few texts are rather complex, but I will try to formulate them in a schematic way (TS texts 264-271) Kumarila has argued that the soul remains the same soul when it experiences first pain, then pleasure and so on, because it continuously contains such qualities as intelligence, tranquility etc. Shantarakshita replies that this cannot be the case. For the Mimamsa insist that the cognizer and what is cognized are non-different: "When one thing is non-different from another, its destruction and origination must follow on the destruction and origination of the latter; just like ...those same States of Happiness and the rest, and the soul has been said to be non-different in nature from the States of Happiness and the rest." (TS text 268 comm.) (For example, it is only if a chair is different from its state of being blue that it can be the same chair if it is painted red. If the chair is non-different from its state of being blue, it must be a different chair if it is painted red. So with the soul. If the soul is one with its state of happiness, it cannot be the same soul if it is in pain. Further, if the soul is one with its states, and the states have a beginning, the soul must have a beginning. But this is contrary to the Mimamsa view that the soul is eternal.)

In TS text 272 Shantarakshita goes back to the central Mimamsa claim that the soul's character of "doer" or "experiencer" is different from any particular state that it is in. Thus, they are claiming that the soul is identical with its character of doer, and is identical with the state it is in, but its character of doing and its particular state are non-identical. Shantarakshita argues that one cannot simply have a "doer". Every doer must be a doer of something. And the doer of 'x' has changed from the doer of 'y'. Jane playing basketball has changed from Jane playing baseball. Kumarila would answer that Jane, as soul or doer, is modified when she stops playing basketball and starts playing baseball; modified but not destroyed. Shantarakshita's reply is subtle. He argues that one cannot disprove that the soul as sentience is eternal. If it were, however, one could not explain why eyes etc. are needed to bring about sentient states. Sentience would exist eternally without them. (TS text 305). The form of sentience is always changing. In this sense the form is destroyed at every moment, and a new form reappears at the next. Jane is inseparable from Jane playing basketball. Jane playing basketball has a definite form, which is destroyed and replaced by the form of Jane playing baseball. All that remains is a formless sentience. If this is all you mean by soul (says Shantarakshita), I have no quarrel with you. The snake can only coil and uncoil because it has no permanent form. The same is true of sentience. If it had a permanent form it could never experience different states.

If there is no soul, that is a soul with a form, where do we get the notion of "I"? Shantarakshita discusses this issue, one of the most important in all of Buddhism, in texts 277-280. It is simply a matter of cause and effect. The "I" notion arises only in some things and not in others - only in those things which have the potential to give rise to it. A jar does not have this potential. A human being has.

The "I" notion is caused to arise but has no real basis. If it did have a basis, that basis would have to be eternal or non-eternal. If it were eternal, all "I" notions would exist together. That is, since the causes of "I" notions were always there, they would all have to be brought about at once. But if the cause is not eternal, yet there was a substantial basis for the "I" notion, we would be able to apprehend it as clearly as those things for which (relatively speaking) there is a real basis. There is color, so we see it. If there were an "I" we would apprehend it. But like Hume, Shantarakshita is saying that we never perceive the self.

To return briefly to the central Mimamsa position that one needs a self or soul to recognize which past and present acts are "one's own" and which are not, Shantarakshita shows that this sort of argument is question begging. One cannot prove the "I" exists by saying that it is necessary in order to recognize the present "I" as the same as the past. But of course, if one does not explain the belief that the "I" endures by the fact that there is an enduring "I," one must find some other way. Shantarakshita locates this in the nature of causality itself. If a momentary state is of such a nature as to give rise to the illusion of a self, plus the illusion that it is the same self as existed before, then one will experience a sense of an enduring self. Why does this happen? Because where sentience exists clinging arises. And the sense of self is a form of clinging. And this produces a karmic chain.

Shantarakshita's next concern is with the Samkhya notion of the soul. The Samkhyas believed that cognition or cosmic intellect was a characteristic of primordial matter alone. *Prakriti* is the producer of all actions, the seed of all evolution. The individual is not a doer at all, but pure passive sentience. (TS texts 285-286) This sentience (or soul) is the enjoyer of the fruit of good or bad deeds. This sentience is one, (one form) changeless and eternal.

Shankaraksita's arguments against this position are similar to those used against the Nyayaika and Mimamsa views, as well as against the doctrine of the *purusha*. If sentience is of one form, how can it perceive diversity? How can it enjoy many different things? How can it desire different things? For perception, enjoyment, desire are either different from sentience, or the same. If the same, then this contradicts the fact that sometimes the soul perceives and enjoys and desires and sometimes it does not. So it would be modified, which contradicts the Samkhya view
.

Further, if as the Samkhyas believe, primordial matter contains all that is and "bestows the fruits in accordance with the desires of the soul," then why do not we always get whatever we want? There is certainly enough in primordial matter to fulfill all desires (TS text 293). And if primordial matter brings about things in accordance with the desires of the soul, how can it be insentient (TS text 299)?

There is no reason, furthermore, to believe that sentience itself is imperishable. Our experience of it is as of something transitory. There is no proof that it cannot be transitory. If it were eternal, one would not need the senses which call it into action. If fire were eternal, we would not need fuel. By analogy if sentience were eternal, we would not need sensation (text 305).

In chapter VI, Shantarakshita offers some friendly criticism of the Advaita (non-dualism) view of the self which he says is substantially correct, with the exception that they hold mind to be eternal. This Hindu view resembles that of Shantarakshita in the following ways: 1) Its adherents assert the world as we know it (relative level) to be of the nature of thought. 2) They deny the reality of the individual self. Shantarakshita does not give the Advaita arguments for these two beliefs, but concentrates on disproving the idea that mind is one and eternal. His first argument follows his general attack on the idea that what is one and eternal can exist in different states. "'In an Eternal Entity there can be no different 'states' because the 'states' are not different from the Entity to which they belong"(TS texts 330-331 comm). Otherwise the eternal entity would be liable to production or destruction which is impossible. And the states cannot be different because this would contradict their view that this eternal entity is all that exists (TS texts 330-332). We cannot know this through inference because a) it is not analytically true that the eternal entity must exist, nor b) are any effects of such an eternal nature discoverable. (TS text 332). This looks as if Shantarakshita is committing a simple mistake. Why can't a single entity exist in different states without failing to remain one? But the Hindu view he is criticizing implies indivisibility in space and changelessness in time. And thus the identity of such a one with itself cannot admit of different states, on their criterion of sameness.

Further, if eternal cognition were all that existed, how could there be the varying states of bondage and liberation? If eternal cognition were eternally right we would already be liberated. If it were eternally wrong, there would be no hope for such liberation. This would make the practice of yoga fruitless. But if cognition is in flux, one's consciousness can change and liberation can be attained (TS texts 333-335).

The next position criticized by Shantarakshita is that of the Pudgalists, an atypical Buddhist sect which held that there is a self but its nature is beyond conception. The orthodox view insists that the self is reducible to the *skandhas* (bundles of body parts, thoughts etc.). Pudgalism arose because some Jain philosophers, fascinated by the teachings of the Buddha, sought to combine them with their own notion of *purusha*. In order to avoid obstacles arising in their practice, Gautama Buddha chose not to take a clear position on the nonexistence of the self. Because of this, some Buddhists believed there was a self, but it was beyond conception. Of course, in Buddhism the *dharmakaya* (the absolute) is beyond conception. And it is possible because it is not provably impossible. On the other hand, self-contradictory things such as the son of a barren woman are not possible. This latter point applies also to the self, which Shantarakshita shows is inconceivable rather than beyond conception. But only those things which are beyond conception are said to be possible which are not provably impossible. The son of a barren woman, for example, is not beyond conception, but impossible, because provably false in virtue of its self-contradictory nature.

The Pudgalists accepted the type of criticism used by Shantarakshita, namely that the self can neither be the same nor different from the momentary thought phases. For this reason, they argued the self must be beyond conception. Yet it must exist, or the Buddha would not have spoken of the "bearer of the burden." Shantarakshita replies that if something cannot be spoken of as being the same or different from something else it must be formless. Because form is exactly that which differentiates. But if. the self is formless it cannot be a substance. (TS texts 340-342) And the Pudgalists utilize conceptions of sameness and difference in talking about the *pudgala*. So it is clear that they mean that it is a substance. (text 343 comm.) Further the reason that the thought phases cannot be the same as the *pudgala* is that they are said by the Pudgalists to have mutually exclusive properties. The thought phases can be spoken of but the pudgala is incapable of being spoken of. (TS text 344)

This argument is followed by another which introduces some very interesting metaphysical ideas. Shantarakshita argues that the *pudgala*, being a substance, must be either eternal or momentary (changing). If eternal, it cannot act, because action implies change and the eternal cannot change. So it must be momentary. (A similar criticism is leveled against Christian theologians by their opponents who claim an eternal unchanging God could not bring the world into existence.)

Shantarakshita then considers an objection of the Pudgalists that

55

the notion of the *pudgala* escapes this criticism, because being beyond conception it cannot be said to be either eternal or noneternal "so effective action cannot be incompatible with it." (TS text 347 comm.)

Shantarakshita here advances an argument which is part of his nominalist bent. He doesn't object to the Pudgalists "calling" the *pudgala* an entity beyond conception, because anything can be called anything. Nevertheless, we can show that their use of this term is incoherent. Because what they mean by "eternal" is that something has a nature which does not change. All they mean by "temporal" is that the nature of a thing changes. So if the Pudgalists accept this notion of the eternal and momentary (to which they do not seem to have objected) then it is clear that they should accept the view that any entity must have either a changing or unchanging nature. But if they accept this, then they cannot also claim that the *pudgala*, an entity, cannot be said to be either eternal or momentary. (TS text 347 comm.)

One might consider at this point whether or not Shantarakshita had any knowledge of Advaita (all is Brahman, distinctions are illusory) philosophers such as Gaudapada who distinguished between the absolute and relative level. For many advaitists (Shankara most notably) true reality was the *Brahman nirgunam*, the Brahman beyond conception. Shantarakshita does not seem to be aware of this position. His criticism of the advaitists seems to ignore their use of the absolute/relative distinction. But if he had known, he might have said (as Kamalashila said of the Pudgalists) that if reality is really beyond conception, then it is meaningless to call it the absolute Brahman or nonBrahman, permanent or impermanent. Of course you can call it Brahman if you like, but then the term Brahman is contentless. For Shantarakshita, the self or "I" is an effect of the momentary causal activity of all the *skandhas* productive of the sense of self. Actually Shantarakshita's position is quite like that of Shankara. I shall return to this later. Shantarakshita has argued that even on the relative level the self does not exist. It is an illusion produced by the skandhas. But what about the *skandhas* themselves? What is their nature, not only with respect to the human person, but all things?

First of all, as Shantarakshita argues in the next chapter, all things are momentary in nature. Nothing whatever can endure through past, present and future time. At first this seems like an outrageous affront to common sense. Surely the flower that one sees when coming into a room is the same one glances at an hour later. But, Shantarakshita argues, this is an illusion. All things which exist must be capable of causing a change in something else or being changed. What exists in one moment of time must produce the next event. For example, the seed, the water, earth, sun, air etc. in one moment of time must produce the first stage of the plant in the next moment of time. If the first moment does not disappear, the next moment cannot come into existence. Thus anything which is non-momentary is fruitless, causally speaking. And to be fruitless is to be nonexistent. (For according to Shantarakshita, to exist is to function.)

It might be argued that ideas, such as beauty, truth, etc. are permanent. Shantarakshita argues that this cannot be, because these words are mere names assigned by whim or habit to groups of things existing in our experience. If we want to call the sun a light and a butter lamp a light we can do so. This does not make them the same thing. If we want to call two similarly appearing momentary successive entities the same thing we can do so. It makes no difference if these entities are thoughts or external things. Calling them the same will not make them the same.

Earlier in the chapter Shantarakshita had argued that things cannot be permanent because of their interdependent nature. Everything is what it is because of certain causal conditions (e.g. the seed, soil etc.) which themselves depend on other things. Shantarakshita is saying that the entire system of existing things is interconnected, so that any change anywhere in the system will sooner or later bring about a change everywhere else. So nothing is self-existing. But, one might argue that the total system is self-existing. Although Shantarakshita does not confront this argument directly, one can see that his subsequent argument about the momentariness of things precludes this possibility. For a totality which must depend at every moment for its existence on the causal conditions of the moment before cannot be said to be self-existing. In short if every moment of time is different from the next and all things are inter-dependent, then nothing can be permanent.

It may be useful now to recall the former objection that if cause and effect are momentary, the cause cannot stay around long enough to touch or bring about the effect, and that if this is so there is no way to explain the invariant concomitance between causes and their effects, e.g. the seed, plus auxiliary conditions, producing the plant and not a chair. The answer to this objection was that what we mean by cause is invariant concomitance. It is simply a name for the orderly way in which we experience reality. As for momentariness itself there is no explanation or cause. It is simply the way reality is.

Theory of Language

In chapter 16, Shantarakshita presents his theory of language which follows directly from his preceding analysis of experience. All of our experience consists in *vijnana* (consciousness), — there are no external objects. Words, therefore, cannot represent objects. How, then, is knowledge possible?

Let us take the word "cow". We have experiences that we call experiences of what is not a cow. "Cow" then, means all that which is not other than cow. It is not an entity. It is a negation. (Shantarakshita follows the logicians, Dignaga and Dharmakirti, in this analysis.)

"This cow" couldn't refer to an entity because the word "cow" is used to mean different cows, and since all is momentary, it would fail to refer twice to the same cow. Nor could it refer to a generality, for these, he has shown, are nonexistent

.

This analysis makes it possible for Shantarakshita to account for our ability to speak meaningfully about unreal entities. (TS texts 1112-1114) For example, there are no blue lotuses. But what we mean by the words "blue lotus" is anything which is not a non-lotus and not non-blue. If there doesn't happen to be any such thing, it doesn't matter. We are still able to say what it is not.

It is obvious that what is implied by this theory of language is a strict relativistic and conventional view of meaning. Words can only be understood in relation to other words.

Although Shantarakshita's position comes from Dignaga and Dharmakirti, it also bears a striking resemblance to the view of the great sixth century Madhyamaka philosopher Chandrakirti. Chandrakirti had insisted on the absolute conventionality of language. As Robert Thurman points out, it is this very insistence on conventionality of meaning that rules out nihilism. For while realizing the complete relativity of our experience we are nevertheless forced to think in conventional terms. We cannot abandon other human beings, responsibilities, pragmatic concerns, philosophical investigation itself. Our very mode of thinking is completely permeated with social reality.

Thurman cites a number of passages from Wittgenstein which highlight the extraordinary similarity between the view of that modern philosopher and Chandrakirti:. (Thurman,pp. 99-100)
"Wittgenstein is most explicit about the sheer conventionality of language, as in the following group of statements:

'The point here is not that our sense impressions can lie, but that we understand their language. (And this language, like any other is founded on convention.') (P.I.(*Philosophical Investigations*) 355)
'One objects: "So you are saying that human agreement decides what is true and what is false?" It is what human beings say that is true and false; and they agree on the language they use. That is not agreement in opinions but in form of life.' (P.I. 241)
Here we strike rock bottom, that is, we have come down to conventions (P.I. 241)

'When philosophers use a word "knowledge","being", "object", "I", "proposition", "name" and try to grasp the essence of the thing, one must always ask oneself: is this word ever actually used in this way in the language-game which is its original home. What we do is to bring the words back from their metaphysical to their everyday use.' (P.I. 116)
'The meaning of a word is its use in the language.' (P.I. 43)
'When I talk about language (words, sentences, etc.) I must speak the language of everyday. Is this language somehow too coarse and material for what we want to say? Then how is another one to be constructed?' (P.I. 120)
A main source of our failure to understand is that we do not command a clear view of the use of our words.' (P.I. 122)

Philosophy can in no way interfere with the actual use of language; it can in the end only describe it. For it cannot give it any foundation either. It leaves everything as it is.' (P.I. 124)
'Essence is expressed by grammar.' (P.I. 371)
'Grammar tells us what kind of object everything is. (P.I. 373)"

Shantarakshita and Chandrakirti do not seem to be in disagreement about the nature of the self. Both believe on the absolute level there is no self but on the level of conventional discourse it is all right to speak as if there were, and as long as one realizes the conventional nature of the designation it does not produce obstacles to enlightenment. Further, both philosophers are objecting to the view that the self is unchanging. Even on the conventional level they believe this to be false.

Why do we call some things "cow" and not others? Shantarakshita answers this question in chapter 17 in terms of perception. When our experience takes a certain shape , our awareness of this shape produces knowledge. We know that it is different from other things and we give it a name. Perception is not the same as knowledge. When we perceive a pot there is a moment of experience that is free from awareness of shape. Our first sight of a pot does not yield understanding of what it is. Perception, therefore, is not knowledge. Naive perception is free from error. (This is an important fact to understand in relation to his view of meditation).

What about the perceptions of enlightened beings? Shantarakshita discusses this problem in chapter 21, when he criticizes the view that entities remain the same throughout the past, present and future. The most important argument is a response to Vasumitra who argued that entities stay the same throughout the three aspects of time, but their relationships change. Their previous condition is called the past, now is called their present and their later condition is now called their future. just as a woman can be called a mother or a daughter depending on her relation to her father or to her son. Shantarakshita argues that for a thing to exist on the relative level it must be able to act (function as an efficient cause) or to be acted on. But the power of action exists only in the present. So no entity can exist in the past or future. (TS text 1842)

At the end of this chapter, Shantarakshita confronts a very interesting objection to the doctrine of the momentariness of entities. If the past and future do not exist, how can emancipated beings know them? The answer sheds a great deal of light on the manner in which the knowledge of an emancipated being is conceived.

"The Mystics cognize that form of the 'Present' thing which directly or indirectly, has become either an effect, or a cause; subsequently, they follow it up with conceptual cognitions, which are purely common (secular) in character, and which are really without objects (without a real, objective background). Thus it is that, on the basis of the said past and future series of causes and effects, proceed all teachings regarding the Past and the Future. As for the Tathagata (Buddha) Himself, His teachings proceed without circumlocution; because the Series of His cognitions are entirely devoid of the webs of Conceptual Context. (TS texts 1853-1856)"

Thus the enlightened meditation master does not actually see an existing future. Rather, consistent with the law of cause and effect and with momentariness, all that is claimed is that his or her insight into the present is so penetrating that the resulting inferences are much more accurate and refined than those of ordinary people. For example, about *The Sutra of the Wise and Foolish*, it is said that the foolish will understand it only as a funny, ironic story about reincarnation, but the wise will learn the lesson that if one wants to learn about one's previous lifetimes one must infer them from one's present situation.

The following analogy may be of use. A retarded child may not understand how someone may be able to say in winter that cherry trees will bloom in the spring. The person who says this is not viewing an already existing future. But rather, he or she knows the patterns of cherry trees. Similarly the enlightened being knows the "patterns" of things and in this sense knows the future. The analogy is limited because the situation of an omniscient being is different for such a person has transcended the illusion of individuality and is thus able to dwell in a state of nonconceptual wisdom. We cannot say what this is of course, but we can benefit from the compassionate manifestation of such a being.

Kamalashila provides us with a further explanation of Buddha's omniscience in his commentary on the *Madhyamakalankara* (*Madhyamakalankarapanjika*). He is answering an argument of the Sarvastivadins that since the Buddha knows past, present and future, the three times must always exist because Buddha cannot know what is false. Kamalashila argues that their permanent existence is not necessary because l the Buddha's veridical knowledge of the three times arises in his awareness moment by moment as if in a dream. This is a result of unimpeded interdependent origination resulting from the absence of obstacles.

The Tathagata's teaching proceeds without circumlocution because his nature has become like the cintamani gem (wish fulfilling jewel) (text 3606-3610). To borrow a metaphor from Coleridge, the activity of the Tathagata is like the Aeolian harp, which plays when the wind blows. Because of the compassion of the Buddha his help spontaneously arises according to the needs of beings, without concept, inference or intention. In the last chapter, Shantarakshita elaborates on the omniscience of the Buddha. The Tathagata, freed from all dualistic thinking, has transcended the distinction between mind and object, self and other. Thus he is able to teach through all his surroundings,- through the universe itself. Admitting there is no direct knowledge of an omniscient Buddha, such a being can be inferred. The Buddha, understanding the nature of reality, has destroyed the poisons and thus, ignorance. These poisons produce all duality and conceptualization which are obstacles to wisdom. Therefore, when these are removed, omniscience should follow. Of course all beings who have achieved buddhahood are properly termed Buddha.

The Buddha knows all things in a single cognition and in a single moment (TS text 3627). This would follow from his transcendence of form, i.e. conceptualization. For it is these forms which impel us to speak of things as having limits, of being x and non x. Once form is transcended, there is no temporal element in awareness.

In his commentary to TS text 3627, Kamalashila mentions an interesting objection to the Buddha's omniscience, namely that it would generate the following paradox. One cannot know everything, because some things like space are limitless. If one were able to mentally encompass space, one's conception would necessarily be false. Kamalashila answers:

"...it is just because He (Buddha) does not apprehend things as limited that He becomes omniscient; otherwise, if He had apprehended the limitless things as limited, He would be clearly mistaken. Because one is called `omniscient' only when He apprehends existing things as existent, and non-existing things as non-existent;- and to the Region of existence, there is no limit at all. Hence if one apprehends as non-existent the limit which does not exist in the form of movement,-and if He apprehends as existent, the Limit, which does exist in the form of being cognised by the Omniscient Person,-why should He be regarded as `Not-Omniscient?"

These considerations concerning omniscient buddhas may indeed seem a bit strange. But turning to the subject of ordinary perception, the problems are just as complex. To begin with, the object of thought must be a compound of objects, because the thought of an object is a result of several internal mental processes. The eye sees the color, the ear hears the sound, etc. The mind binds these experiences together and tells us that they all belong to the same object. (Even in terms of one sense, e.g. sight, we see different parts of an object successively. we see the head of a tall man, then his shoulders etc. But consciousness makes these things appear to us in such a way as if we were experiencing them all at once.) The image of the tall man across the room enters our visual field as a tiny figure less than an inch in height. Yet our minds make the necessary changes for us, and we perceive such a person to be the same height he would be if he were directly in front of us. Perspective, in other words, is automatically factored in for us.

But if we assume that the parts of the object, the uncompounded object, are the reality beneath the appearance we also run into trouble. Suppose we take the position that the objects of thought are atoms. As already pointed out, atoms are supposed to be indivisible elements. But anything which exists must have sides: to put it in terms relative to the earth, there is a north, south etc. But if atoms are simple and indivisible this cannot be. So how can atoms exist? If the atoms are empty in nature, how can objects be composed of them? Modern physics is also concerned with this problem. Atoms, even today, are considered so unpredictable and ephemeral in nature no one can explain how reality can be composed of them.

An article in Scientific American described the work of a think tank at Stanford in which scientists were seriously proposing the idea that elementary particles. ought not to be considered either one nor many,—reminiscent of Shantarakshita. (Mukerjee,p. 72)

What remains then, is our subjective knowledge of the world. But how can the external world and the subjective world be the same? One can know one's own experience directly, but not that of others. Descartes argued that the self can know only itself with certainty. Everything else is in doubt.

The effect follows the cause in an orderly, predictable way (e.g. plant a marigold seed in good soil with light and water and you get a marigold) because both "cause" and "effect" originate from consciousness. Of course they do not originate in most cases from the individual consciousness alone. If that were the case we could make wine out of water. Sometimes the individual consciousness does function as cause as, for example, when we write a poem. But cases such as the marigold seed producing the marigold come from the ocean of consciousness which Shantarakshita calls *vijnana*.

Ego clinging distorts the *vijnana* and produces a stream of consciousness immersed in suffering. Liberated consciousness sees itself as one with the totality, and being selfless, does not suffer. Although Shantarakshita does not say this we might speculate that if reality were composed of mostly enlightened minds we would have a paradise and if mainly unenlightened minds, a hell. One might rightly object that if the *alaya vijnana* is itself momentary, it cannot explain invariant concomitance. Why does one mental moment bring about the next in an orderly way? Why is the suffering consciousness of a bereaved lover at time (1) followed by suffering consciousness of this lover at time (2)? Why couldn't it just as well be followed by joy? To explain it by karma would beg the question because karma is just a form of causality. Shantarakshita does not give us an answer to this question. All states, psychic and physical, plant their seeds at one moment and the results are reaped the next, in an orderly way.

The Madhyamakalankara and the
Madhyamakalankaravrtti
Let us now turn to the *Madhyamakalankara* MA and the

Madhyamakalankaravritti MAV. The argument proceeds in a single way leading to a dual conclusion. All things whatever fall into the category of one or many. These are exhaustive and inclusive. An argument is advanced in one case after another to show that the object in question cannot be one or many. Therefore the object is non-existent. The incoherence of the concept of an external (non-mental) object, either compounded or uncompounded, is demonstrated. Consciousness is left as the only alternative, and the substantial non duality of subject and object once shown to be feasible, leaves consciousness in possession of the field, at least on the relative level. On the absolute level, which is free from the concepts of one or many, subject, object, one cannot even say reality is mind (consciousness). In this way Shantarakshita unifies the views of Nagarjuna and Asanga. The MAV is Shantarakshita's own commentary on his root text.

Shantarakshita begins by arguing that nothing can be permanent. He means this in the strong sense that everything is momentary. Each moment of time seems to be connected with the next as its cause. Yet only one moment exists at a time. It follows that each point in the causal process is instantaneous. So cause and effect cannot really be connected. Shantarakshita follows Nagarjuna on this point.

Shantarakshita continues with an attack on materialism. All of material reality must be either single or compound. It cannot be single for the following reason:

> 10. Since they are connected in many directions,
>   How could pervading things be one?
>   And also since parts are covered or not covered,
>   Then gross things cannot possibly be one.
>   Nor can there be a manifold of partless atoms.
>
> 11. If connected or else surrounded,
>   Or even completely (inseparable) with no gap,
>   A single partless atom is embedded in other atoms,
>   And faces another atom.

12. But if one says that they face one another and are partless,
    They would be the same.
    In this case, would they not fail to
    Become earth, water and so on?

14. Each particle is thus proved to be without inherent nature.
    Therefore the eye, substance, etc. (composed of atoms),
    About which my own schools and others have much to say,
    Should be understood as having no intrinsic nature.

Rang rig

Rang rig, or self awareness is one of the thorniest problems in Buddhist philosophy. From the very start, Buddhists rejected the idea of an unchanging soul or self. In the early writings, a person is said to be a mere collection of *skandhas* (form, sensation feeling, thoughts, and consciousness). But traditionally, all activities such as perceiving etc. were analyzed in terms of subject, object and activity. For example, "John plays ball" or "Jane sees the cat." What about the 'I' in "I am self aware"? What is the I that knows what I am doing? What is it to be aware of what I am doing?

From the very start, Shantarakshita asserts in his MAV that awareness is appropriately attributed to a sentient being, and not to an object like a stone:

16. Consciousness must arise
    From what excludes non-sentience,
    That is from what
    Has the nature of knowledge

17. Because its nature is unique and partless,
    It is impossible for it to have a threefold nature.
    Therefore self-awareness does not have
    The property of subject and object, [and activity].

Consequently (the early philosophers say) the object of knowledge is able to establish its own aspect. It is a cause and can elicit knowledge of its own form. And consciousness of the nature of the stipulated object is produced. Thus the knower, the known, and the manner of knowing together are produced by the object which is said to be like this in its own nature. But self- awareness cannot be established as an object in this way. Because generating by itself a partless consciousness, it is not the producer, the producing, or what is produced. In this manner, the knower, the knowing and known are not different modes of awareness perceived in the threefold way. (MAV)

18. This is the nature of consciousness.
    Thus self-understanding is possible.
    But how could it know the nature of objects if
    As you have asserted, the nature of objects is different
    [from consciousness]?

19. Since its nature does not exist in [external] objects,
    Because you have asserted
    That subject and object are different,
    How could consciousness know that which is other [than
    consciousness]?

> Since its nature does not exist in [external] objects,
> Because you have asserted
> That subject and object are different
> Having this characteristic,
> Ultimately [consciousness and its object] will
> remain separated. —TS

20. The features [of subject and object] in your theory
Appear to be different in substance from each other.
But their reflection is similar, being both aspects
of mind.
And the conventional distinction is, in a sense,
tied on conventionally. (MAV)

The issue of self reflexive awareness is of lively interest today. In 2006 there was a debate at the American Philosophical Association between Jay Garfield and Paul Bernier with Raziel Abelson commenting. It was clear from the discussion that there were different ways in which Shantarakshita's views could be interpreted. Can modern science be of help here?

Recently, cognitive scientists have identified parts of the brain which "tell" us the "difference" between perceptions. imagination, memories, dreams etc. And the brain also identifies an experience as mine, rather than someone else's. When these markers are disturbed by Alzheimer's, LSD etc. we don't get the same messages.

I think Shantarakshita is saying that causal conditions result in experiences marked as ours or others. In other words, self reflexive awareness is not an awareness of the self, but just a type of awareness that we have under certain conditions. Georges Dreyfus in a lecture at Columbia University's School of Religious Studies, January 25, 2008 said something similar, namely that there is something about experience that makes you know it is yours. My guess is that is all Shantarakshita meant by self- cognition.
To summarize: Shantarakshita is rejecting the view that the objects of knowledge are distinct substances existing apart from the mind. Shantarakshita by rejecting extra-mental reality, is following

Vasubandhu on these points, refuting the Vaishesika view that we know objects directly and these objects are composed of atoms, as well as the Sautrantika view that atoms produce reflections in our minds when we perceive them, and these reflections are the object of knowledge.

Shantarakshita accepts self awareness, but says this is not an awareness of an object. Subject and object are epistemologically distinguishable, but ontologically inseparable.

In his excellent analysis of Shantarakshita's position MA and MAV, James Blumenthal points out that the Tibetan commentator Gyel-tsab misinterprets Shantarakshita's position on self-awareness:

"Shantarakshita appears to be addressing his argument here to an opponent who holds that consciousness is partless and truly singular while accepting self-cognizing cognition, but at the same time wishes to assert the existence of objects which are utterly distinct from or external to the consciousness perceiving them. Both the idea of a unified undifferentiated mind and the objects external to the mind are unacceptable tenets according to Shantarakshita. Thus, he seems to have two aims here: the first is to demonstrate that no such truly singular mind exists; secondly, he wants to convince such an opponent that objects are not utterly distinct from the consciousness perciving them. Gyel-tsab's commentary seems to zero in on the rejection of external objects but not on the rejection of a truly singular self-cognizing cognition. While Shantarakshita would certainly be pleased to have convinced an opponent to accept self-cognizing cognition, this is still occurring within the framework of his much larger Madhyamaka argument aimed at demonstrating that all entities lack a truly existent nature because they lack either a singular or manifold nature, a point Gyel-tsab seems to have lost sight of here. "

Santaraksita continues with an analysis of Buddhist views on perception with which he disagrees.

The Vaibhasika theory of perception

The Vaibhasika were naïve realists, believing that we had direct knowledge of the object of perception which was composed of atoms. The object of perception is not only distinguishable but is also separable from the mind.

> 21. For those who do not assert that consciousness
>   Is transformed by the aspect of the object,
>   Then (in their system), there would be no knowledge
>   Of the existence of the external object. (MAV)

Shantarakshita argues against this view for the following reason. Because the object of knowledge is by nature unknowable, one's object of awareness is distanced from the object itself. It is not correct to attach a label. If this is so, it is not correct to say that the object in itself can correlate with consciousness. This cannot be the case. (MAV)

Shantarakshita is pointing out that the partless atoms, themselves devoid of features such as color etc. cannot account for how objects appear to our minds, with all their   richness and diversity,

Sautrantika theories of perception

There are three versions of the Sautrantika understanding of perception. All are predicated on the idea that one can only perceive in the present, and that the present moment is an indivisible instant. These alternative views are as follows: 1) One unified mental state grasps the reflected object all at once, as for example, when one perceives a flowered cup, 2) (Half-egg:- Single aspects of the object are successively grasped by matching single mental states) One perceives a single aspect of the reflected object (e.g. a bit of green leaf) then another and another, but so quickly it is like a torch that is whirled about producing the illusion of a circle of light. This is how one seems to see the flowered cup all at once when it really happens gradually. The borders of the perceptions are joined by memory, 3) A number of mental states equal to the number of aspects of the reflected object grasp all the aspects in a single instant.

Shantarakshita criticizes these views in the following way:

1) One mental state, many aspects; The argument that a single unified mental state cannot be of a manifold is affirmed. It cannot be of a manifold without diversifying and losing its singularity:

> 22. [If you claim] one cognition is not many,
>   There cannot be many images.
>   But then the view of mind as a unity
>   Has no power to establish many objects.

2) Half egg: If one perceives aspect by aspect successively, the resulting state of awareness would be illusory rather than a veridical perception. The circle of light made by the mind is not really there. There is only the torch in different places. Nor can this be a memory. Memories are less clear and bright than the circle of light one seems to see. (Modern psychologists would describe the circle of light as an image produced by various causes in the brain). Further, if perceptions appeared so quickly as to seem simultaneous, how could we tell the difference between hearing *tala* (banana tree) and *lata* (vine)? They would sound the same. Rather we are aware of successive sounds.

3) Many mental states, many aspects:: Shantarakshita argues that if perception involved a manifold of mental states equal in number to the aspects of the object which they contacted, then to explain how we saw the whole object, we would need an infinite number of mental states at every instant of perception, since the perceived reflected object is infinitely divisible by the mind. In MAV, Shantarakshita goes further, stating that the mind knows all sides of the object, even those not directly visible. So a direct connection would be problematic:

> 32. In that case, how could whiteness and so forth,
>   Which are known in a single way,
>   Have differences, such as a top, middle and bottom?
>   Each of these would have to become distinct objects
>   of knowledge [which is absurd].

Thus similarly, blue and white, etc., are compound objects which are asserted to be one, have opposite sides and a great number, and a top [Height , length and width-three dimensional] and these parts of objects one knows to be manifold . If so, how is it understood to be one [object]? Or having asserted a manifold, one only grasps a small particle without branches [atomic], then in that case, having distinguished with certainty the divisions of each of the aspects of these branches of the object [which are infinitely divisible], this [infinite manifold]cannot be perceived even by those with very subtle insight. MAV
This view is not experiential. (MAV)"

> 33. A bit of white etc., atomic in nature
> In itself, single and partless,
> Which appears to anyone's consciousness,
> I do not feel [Tib. *Tsor*] exists.

Even concentrating my mind, I do not see a partless atom. But you, without seeing it, deceive yourself by accepting it. The reason that intelligent people have for accepting something as existing is that they can perceive it. Since this [partless image] is not perceptible, it is not correct [to assert its existence]. Just as many-colored butterflies are not one, so to designate [these bits of color for example] as one, is not correct. Thus designating aspects of consciousness as one, which are not one, is not acceptable.(MAV)"

Shantarakshita also argues that if the object of mind were so completely different from our perception of it, we could never be assured of veridical knowledge. Thus Shantarakshita rejects all of the Sautrantika views of perception. He also rejects a number of non-Buddhist views that reality is one and indivisible, interrupting his critique of Buddhist views of perception to do so. Some realist philosophers had argued that one of the elements, (earth, or air etc.) was the only substance. But these philosophers had also claimed that direct perception was the only veridical knowledge. Their view is inconsistent because one cannot know through direct perception that all is air, or fire etc. (See *sloka* 37.) Nor can it be consistently argued as it was with the Samkhyas, that the three qualities (brightness, force, mass) are reducible to a single principle of nature. For if nature is one, it cannot be manifested as many, or inconsistency would be an essential part of reality, and we could never know it.

Shantarakshita is however, equally critical of the Chittamatra view of Vasubandhu that mind is ultimate reality. For mind is not knowable as an object. Consciousness is pure subjectivity. (*sloka* 18)

But what is the nature of consciousness, and what are its objects? Shantarakshita considers two Chittamatra views, one of which can be further divided into three types. The first view holds that subject and object are one. That is, there is no distinction between the knowing mind and its object. And since all distinctions are imaginary, mind must be indivisible . All that occurs is a result of the maturing habits or tendencies of this mind.

According to Shantarakshita, mind cannot be one, because what it knows is many. If, as some argue, subject and object are identical, and objects are manifold, then mind would be as well .

Some argue that the distinct mental objects are not separate from the subject that knows them. While agreeing that subject and object cannot be distinct substances, Shantarakshita replies that if they were identical, we could not learn about events sequentially. We would learn everything all at once. For temporal divisions imply disunity. Not even a magic trick can fake this.

Even if reality were really one, our names for it are distinct. And these names are made up of letters. So we do know at least that these are distinct objects.

It is generally correct that, although mind is a manifold, we do know what appears to our minds (sense impressions) as images rather than material objects. There are three forms of this view and they follow the divisions of the Sautrantika theories.
(a) Some have argued that there are two aspects to mind (half egg theory). Although from the absolute point of view (pure consciousness) all is one mind, from the relative point of view, there are

minds and distinct objects. Like a split hard-boiled egg, each perception is half mind, half object. Shantarakshita rejects this, because it is a contradiction to say that the same mind can be both one and many. If this were the case, all opposites, moving, not moving, before, after, would be the same, which would be very hard to accept as true. (4648) Further, these philosophers believe we perceive one aspect of a thing at a time. But this cannot account for the fact that we can perceive some things to be hot and others to be cold simultaneously.

(b) Shantarakshita considers another form of idealism held by some Buddhists, namely that each person has many minds knowing many mental images. (This resembles a modern view that there is a separate part of the brain that identifies different aspects, such as shape, color, etc.). If, as Buddhists, they have rejected the idea of an unchanging mind, then there is a separate mind for each individual aspect at every instant. And everything that exists must be held in existence by a separate act of consciousness. So there would have to be a separate mind (thought) for each of these. But we are aware of no such thing. (*sloka* 49)

"As Mipham states:
But when the Chittamatrins say that there are as many cognitions as there are mental aspects, consciousness, which in their view is truly existent, cannot be established. When something appears as multiple, each of its many aspects is also perceived as possessed of parts in terms of spatial direction (center, extremities, etc.). In other words, each aspect has many parts, in just the same way as when the infinitesimal particle is investigated. The Chittamatrins cannot say that such an investigation applies only to the particles and not to consciousness... Therefore it is said that it is hard to sidestep such an investigation-indeed it is impossible to do so."
—(Padmakara,2005, p.244)

(c) Some believe that distinct objects are just a reflection of one continuous mind; objects are perceived to be different, but really are of a single nature. But if this were the case we would have no explanation for why distinctions arose in the first place. d) Some believe that there really are no objects, not even mental ones, and the perception of objects is a mistake. But this is contrary to common sense. What we call mental has quite different qualities from what we call physical. Further, things certainly appear to be different from each other. Mental states, for example, such as happiness and unhappiness are not the same. Are all these distinctions an illusion? If this were the case we could not know anything at all.

How all forms of idealism ultimately fail
If there is nothing but mind, how can awareness of objects arise in the mind? This must be caused and so the causal conditions which produce awareness in the individual mind must exist apart from that mind. Otherwise it would have no experience. It is dependent for experience on causal conditions:

> 60. Then if you think all cognitions are illusory,
>   How is this illusion perceived?
>   If images arise in the mind by the power of this illusion,
>   Then it is still the power of another. "

As a result of this investigation Shantarakshita concludes that all things, including the individual mind, are dependent on other things. (interdependent co-origination) . Nothing can exist independently of other things. Not even the individual mind is self sufficient.

So we know things, he concludes, in an artificial way. We seem to know them as if they were independent things, - chairs, tables, etc. But on closer examination we see this is impossible. Our awareness is held in existence by interdependent causal conditions which are beyond our ken. We only see the result, like a mirage. We see the chair and the table but not their real nature. As mentioned before, Dennett, the Churchlands and others have pointed out that the mind is not unlike a computer with a program that is interpreting our experience. Shades of "The Matrix"!

The very notion of existence and nonexistence is a category imposed by the mind. Ultimate reality admits of no distinctions, of no theories etc. We can say nothing about it. Thus holding no theory, Shantarakshita eludes criticism. (67-71 MA)

68. Those who do not assert anything to be existent or
    nonexistent
    Nor both existent and nonexistent,
    Not even very diligent opponents
    Can successfully criticize.

As Mipham Rinpoche says in his commentary to the MA *sloka* 66:
(Doctor, 2004, p.481)

"To the minds of immature beginners, emptiness and appearance
or existence or nonexistence inevitably seem as if they were mutually exclusive, with one being the negation of the other. It is hard
to realize how these form a union. Nevertheless, when the vase
placed in front [of us] is investigated with the reasoning of one and
many, it is seen to be, in essence, devoid of even a particle of established nature. That emptiness is not something that did not exist
before and has only now occurred at the time of investigating.
Therefore, although it appears to arise, cease and disintegrate, the
vase has not moved in the slightest from the state empty of nature.
While being empty, it appears as it does, and so one must develop
certainty that the actual condition is one of appearance and emptiness united. Generally emptiness is easily realized through the
meaning of absence of truth, but trust in the way that emptiness
arises as independent origination is hard to arrive at. Once that has
been reached, the foundation of the view for all Sutra and Mantra
has been laid down."

To be convinced that things, the bases of appearances, are
"untrue," inasmuch as they are without inherent existence, and to
see how dependently arising appearances manifest infallibly, is the
greatest of all wonders. It is to this that the present stanza alludes:

Concerning those views about existence
Non-existence and neither both existence nor non-existence,
It would be a long time
Before you could challenge on this point one that has no position.
                                        —Aryadeva, *Four Hundred Views*

At this point Shantarakshita changes his approach. Having argued that reality is beyond conception, he raises the question as to why people can not directly perceive it nonconceptually. He concludes that it must be because consciousness is obscured by habits of categorization and evaluation, tendencies due to karma and environment. (73-74) So what hope is there that anyone will attain absolute awareness? Shantarakshita claims this is possible through the attainment of yogic perception through meditation. (75) This is possible because the absolute and relative levels are ways of intuiting the same reality, - one pure, one impure. Reason can show the necessity of going beyond ordinary knowledge because it can show that ordinary knowledge is confused. Similarly, sense experience, purified, leads, through yogic meditation, to pure awareness.

The relative level, then is of great value, it is not to be rejected. If, on the relative level, one removes the causal conditions producing obscurities,, they will disappear and the true nature will be attained. (82-87)

So the idealists are correct to argue that the relative level has the nature of mind.

> 91. Causality
>   Is also only mind.
>   Whatever is established by the mind,
>   Remains mind.

However, one can see that phenomena including mind have no independent reality. This suggests the Madhyamakas are right that the ultimate nature of reality is emptiness.
Yongey Mingyur Rinpoche has an insightful comment to make on the 'matrix' aspect discussed above:

"I can't think of a better example of the patience and diligence required to really recognize your true potential, your true Buddha nature, than the first in the series of Matrix movies, which many of you probably saw years before I did. The movie impressed me not only because the conventional reality experienced by people caught up in the Matrix was eventually revealed as an illusion, but also because even with the benefit of all the equipment and training available to him, it still took the main character, Neo, a while to recognize that the personal limitations he'd accepted for most of his life were in fact only projections of his own mind. Are subject and object the same or different?"

—(Mingyur Rinpoche)

At first sight, there seems to be a contradiction between what Shantarakshita says in the *Tattvasamgraha* and the *Madhyamakalankara* about the duality or non-duality of mind and object. In the *Tattvasamgraha* he argues against those who say there must be a separate unchanging self who is the knower of the object. Among his many arguments against this view is the infinite regress charge that to know the substantial self demands another knower, and so on. In the *Madhyamakalankara,* he argues that subject and object cannot be the same because they cannot be either one or many, the same or different. He bases this on his critique of what he believes to be all possible views of the relation between the subject and the perceived object.

So what is Shantarakshita's view about subject and object? An analogy with the dancer and the dance may be helpful. The dancer while dancing and the dance are distinguishable but not separable. The subject is not a thing existing apart from its object. But it is distinguishable from the object in many ways. These ways are determined by context; by the situations in which the personal pronoun "I" is used. This does not mean that the "I" is unchanging. The dancer changes along with the dance.

Since the objects of knowledge are all mental in nature, on the relative level, subject and object can be said to be equally mental. For surely the subject is as mental as anything can be. So on the relative level, Shantarakshita is an idealist. But on the absolute level idealism itself is inadequate, for mind itself, being a concept, cannot be non-relativistically real.

There are, therefore, two levels of relative truth. On the rough, everyday common sense level, there are knowers and objects of knowledge. These appear to be separable, but on closer examination objects are discovered to be forms of thought. Only on the absolute level is thought itself discovered to be empty in nature As summarized in Ven. Khenchen Palden Sherab Rinpoche's and Khentrul Tsewang Dongyal Rinpoche's commentary on the *Madhyamakalankara:*

A) Relative Level (Unanalyzed)
"On this level it is correct to make distinctions between real and unreal, hot and cold, table and chair, large objects and atoms etc. These concepts form a network of meaning in which each term depends on others for its usefulness to us."

B) Relative Level (Analyzed)
When we examine external reality closely, we discover that terms like atom, matter, elements, make no sense. Nor does the notion of a single element such as nature make sense. But internal reality is in no better shape. The notion of one mind is incoherent; but so is the notion of many minds.

It is also impossible to maintain that the mind depends on nothing else. If this were the case we could not account for the orderly arising of thoughts. So there is interdependent co-origination. Mind depends on this.

Nor is it possible to deny awareness. To do so is self contradictory, because there must be awareness to deny awareness. So on the Pure Relative Level, one can assert the reality of awareness and interdependent co-origination.

C) Impure Ultimate Level
On closer examination, however, we discover two truths:
1) Given Nagarjuna's critique of causality, inter-dependent co-origination is itself an incoherent concept.
2) Given the fact that awareness is pure subjectivity, it can never be known directly as an object. So it is unknowable.
 D) Pure Absolute Truth: Reality is beyond conception. We call it emptiness."

Skepticism

Near the end of the *Madhyamakalankara*, Shantarakshita faces the paradox of skepticism. On the absolute level, he wants to maintain that nothing can be known as true. But how can he express this without asserting a fact about knowledge? He does so by refusing to assert anything as true. Therefore there is nothing for anyone to refute.(*sloka* 68)

Shantarakshita has not rejected ordinary truth on the functional (pragmatic) level:

> On the relative level, I did not reject
> Either the relations of cause and effect between entities
> Or categories of *samsara* and *nirvana* etc.
> These concepts should not be mixed up on the relative level.
> Since we can classify things in terms of cause and effect,
> And characterize phenomena in general on the relative level,
> The accumulation path can exist in a pure state.
>
> Thus from the point of view of the middle way all
>   phenomena are useful
> And useful in gaining enlightenment, for,
> By means of a completely pure cause
> A completely pure effect arises. (MA *slokas* 84-86)"

At this point I will defer to Ven. Khenchen Palden Sherab Rinpoche's and Khentrul Tsewang Dongyal Rinpoche's excellent commentary:

"Starting with verse sixty-three, he puts aside his discussion of the absolute level and turns his attention to the relative. The relative level has three main characteristics. It seduces the mind into accepting reality, because 1) on an unexamined level it looks perfectly convincing. 2) It is constantly changing, as instant by instant it disappears and is replaced by the arising of the next instant. Nothing is permanent,—phenomena are an endless stream of birth and death. All that exists is functional,—that is, anything real functions as a cause in the system of interdependent co-origination. This stream of causes stretches endlessly into the future. Every result comes about in this way, relying on causes immediately before it. So that is all you can say about the relative level, that is, that it is constantly changing in accordance with cause and effect, and when you analyze even this, you find its nature is emptiness. Other than this, Shantarakshita has no opinion about it. So there is nothing to refute in his system. On the ultimate level, existence and non-existence are categories which do not apply, for this level is beyond distinctions...." (Sherab and Dongyal, forthcoming)

In MA *sloka* 70, (Shantarakshita) forestalls a possible criticism that he can say nothing about the absolute level at all, since it is beyond conception. He points out that there is nevertheless some similarity between what he says and the absolute level, because the absolute level is beyond distinctions and complexities, and his method of reasoning breaks down distinctions and complexities. Further, there are two levels of the absolute, one of which is accessible in accordance with the capabilities of ordinary people. One of these ordinary ways to the absolute is through reasoning,—another way lies through selfless virtue and devotion. The only way to the higher absolute level is beyond ordinary capabilities, for it involves the spontaneous opening of the wisdom mind.
One might object that one cannot have it both ways. If the real ultimate is beyond words, then one simply cannot speak of it at all. As Wittgenstein says in the *Tractatus*, "Of what one cannot speak one must be silent." Thus what sense can be given to a "proximate ultimate"?

In answer to this question, I can only offer a solution of my own, which helps me to make sense of this notion. The absolute and the relative knowledge of emptiness cannot be directly compared. But what can be compared is one's experience of the relative and one's experience of the ultimate. Many of the great masters have asserted that the experience of the absolute is the source of waves of compassion, wisdom and bliss. Similarly those on the path experience greater and greater wisdom, compassion and bliss as they progress. While ultimate experience is not the same as relative, there is some similarity between the compassion, wisdom and bliss experienced in both. Experiences in short, can be compared. Of course one must be enlightened to know this. But even an unenlightened person can venture to accept the ultimate as a sort of hypothetical construct that accounts for the power and goodness of the buddhas. Further, it is this similarity between relative and absolute bliss that forms the basis of Shantarakshita's argument in the *Tattvasiddhi*.

The Tattvasiddhi

The *Tattvasamgraha* and *Madhyamakalankara* are philosophical masterpieces on the level of relative truth. In the *Tattvasiddhi*, Shantarakshita explains how the tantra leads to the absolute level. His argument unfolds in terms of ethics and logic. The central issue which Shantarakshita confronts is the Theravada (Hinayana) and Mahayana teachings that desires are defilements and obstacles to enlightenment. Shantarakshita does not deny the truth of this teaching on the ordinary level. But he argues that a realized person, because of his or her egolessness, can transform the poison of desire and attachment into the nectar of liberation. He also argues that this is not contrary to the teachings of the Buddha who is quoted in *The Heap of Jewels Sutra* as having said that the rubbish of the city can be used as manure in the sugar cane and grape fields. What justification does Shantarakshita offer for this position?

His argument follows directly from his metaphysical analysis which he presented in the *Tattvasamgraha* and the *Madhyamakalankara*. It is the mind which imposes form and categories on reality. The most pernicious of these forms are the categories of self and other. The idea of self, produced through ignorance, gives rise to the poisons of anger, hatred, greed, jealousy and fear. These distort our vision of reality and poison our world. If this process is reversed, by tantric practice involving *mantra* and *mudra* (a ritual physical posture), the poisonous aspect of experience is eliminated. But this purified response to experience does more than just eliminate poison. It allows us to achieve awareness on the absolute level.

Let us go back to our central analogy for understanding *tantra*, the relation between aesthetic experience and ordinary experience.

Imagine a painter, perhaps Ingres, who is entranced with the beauty of the female body. His appreciation is both sensual and loving. He does not see it as a symbol, (of God for example), but as beautiful, quite heavenly, in its own nature. Such a painter in his day horrified and frightened ordinary people who saw in his enraptured acceptance of erotic sensuality an invitation to a low form of unbridled lust and the cruelty which often accompanies it. But now most educated people realize that Ingres' appreciation of the nude body was aesthetic rather than a mere desire for a sexual release. This does not mean that Ingres necessarily did not feel sexual passion as he painted his models. It means rather that this passion was transformed into a vision of the aesthetic qualities of the figure as well as a sharing of his experience with those of his audience capable of aesthetic response.

To repeat a point made earlier, aesthetic qualities are linked to, but not reducible to other types of qualities such as physical qualities. An example is balance in a painting. A balanced painting evokes in us a feeling somewhat akin to seeing a dancer balancing *en pointe*, or, more prosaically, a construction worker balancing on a beam. But balance in a painting transcends the physical origins of the meaning of the word. It is also non-reducible in terms of the elements of the painting itself. For example symmetry may produce balance or its opposite. It depends on the use of color, perspective, even subject matter. Aesthetic qualities may even depend on the context in which the work of art is placed. If a simple box-like structure is placed in a concentration camp it may appear quite different than if placed in a garden.

Similarly, the enlightened person may be said to experience reality from a special perspective. One can use words such as wisdom, compassion and bliss within this perspective, but to at least some extent they acquire new meanings. The enlightened person has realized his or her connection with all things, and in a timeless way. So there need not be any clinging or attachment of any kind to any part of experience. All is enjoyed in a state of equanimity. And compassion spontaneously arises in the form of activity designed to share this bliss with all beings.

We can understand the difficulty the great teachers have in explaining this mode of experience to ordinary people if we consider how difficult it would be to explain aesthetic experience to someone completely devoid of it. Aesthetic awareness is a higher perspective on life, - to understand it one must share it. Fortunately most, perhaps all human beings have some understanding of such aesthetic qualities as beauty, grace, vitality etc. Through study and experience such perception is enhanced. Vajrayana Buddhists believe that all sentient beings have at least a dim awareness of their own enlightened nature. This seed of enlightenment is called the *tathatagarbha*. So through study and experience they can be led to an appreciation of the true nature of things in a way analogous to how someone can deepen appreciation of art. Or they may "recover their aesthetic sight" as someone with hysterical blindness can be cured.

To return now to the analysis of *mantra* (a sound, syllable or group of word the purpose of which is spiritual realization) and *mudra* (a gesture of the body, usually of the hands, for religious purposes), Shantarakshita says in the *Tattvasiddhi* that these are the means of achieving the transformation of experience from the level of the ordinary to that of realization. There are particular *mantras* and *mudras* which are designed to heighten awareness. Because of their special qualities, they are able to help people to see all of experience as *mudra* and *mantra*; i.e. as manifestations of wisdom / emptiness / skillful means. For example the *mudra* of the open hand of generosity can, combined with a sense of egolessness, induce in us a feeling as if being itself were generous. The mantra spoken with devotion and a sense of formlessness, opens one to the feeling that all sounds are the sounds of the Buddha. In this way experience is raised to a higher perspective as the fruit of a sour fruit tree, which has been grown from seeds soaked in milk, becomes sweet.

One might argue that the heightening of experience can be done more safely within the realm of monastic discipline. Why does the tantric practitioner have to become involved with such apparently troublesome aspects of experience as desire and furious wrathful deities? But would it not be shortsighted to tell a great painter or playwright to look only at the pretty side of life and ignore the rest? If an artist were to follow such a foolish course, how could he or she bring about the aesthetic transformation of the tragic and ugly side of life? Similarly if duality is to be overcome, all of life must be embraced and transformed. There are no exceptions. And the difficult, disgusting and horrible are challenges to the *Tantrayana* practitioner.

The *bodhisattva* wishes for the unexcelled happiness of all beings. But such happiness cannot possibly be achieved through penance, through the *bodhisattva's* self-torment. Only through happiness and gladness can one achieve Buddhahood. (folio 56) This absolute nature cannot be described in words, but because it is experienced as perfect bliss, it is not completely incorrect to describe the source of this experience as perfect bliss. And because those who achieve this experience manifest wisdom and compasion, it seems not incorrect to say that the source is similar to wisdom and compassion. And thus it seems appropriate to think of the source the way we think of a compassionate, wise and blissful person, that is, as Dharmakaya Buddha.

Yet it is important to remember that Shantarakshita asserts that the ultimate is beyond duality. We are not speaking of a God that encompasses all things. The *dharmakaya* is neither identical with the totality nor different. It transcends all categories such as subject and object. It is neither one nor many.

The world of appearances then cannot be rejected in favor of a cosmic other. Appearances are just as much Buddha as the ultimate. They are indissoluble. Thus: By the process of transformation of perception the yogi can use the world of forms to produce great happiness. Just as an object cannot be both hot and cold at the same time and in the same way, so a being cannot at the same time be both completely happy and unhappy. Through one's practice,that is through the combination of meditation (wisdom/emptiness) and compassion skillful means) one can become completely and unchangingly happy. *Tattvasiddhi*:
"Striving diligently for bodhichitta, how should the yogi achieve this transformation? By abandoning the ego completely. And not through the torments of asceticism. How else but through bliss will one attain bliss? Why is this the case? This is because the bodhisattva's mind has become naturally luminous. This luminos-

ity arises from nonattachment to form. Where there is no attachment to form, there can be no suffering. The mind on the absolute level is in a state of equanimity no matter what circumstances arise. In the Theravada and Mahayana traditions, this detachment is achieved through duality or opposites. The antidote for illusion is meditation on dependent arising. The antidote for lust is meditation on the repulsiveness of the human body. In Vajrayana, however, one achieves detachment through desires. Or, to put it in another way, through the practice of skillfulmeans and wisdom. The bodhisattva \uses \the \world of forms to go beyond both attachment and non-attachment: Sentient beings, having been brought into the great path, must understand that many different causes in combination bring about (different) results. The cause of knowledge of egolessness will result in a person never being burdened with attachments. There is no other way to gain this great happiness. Because of this food, all activities will be transformrd into great bliss. Because do not people become similar to what possesses them? How in any other manner could a person become transformed? (Folio 56) Relying on this practice for the purpose of obtaining nectar, we can turn these very poisons into nectar. So it was said in the *Ratnakara Sutra*. For example, Buddha said:

Kàsyapa, the manure of the big cities if used by the farmer will be put to good use in the sugar cane and grape fields. So it is said.

And thus, Kàsyapa, similarly the Bodhisattva uses the manure of his defilements to produce benefits leading to omniscience.

Buddha also said:
Oh Kàsyapa, people protected by mantra and medicine, even when they take poison will not die, So similarly, those bodhisattvas, protected by wisdom and skillful means, will completely terminate the poison of emotions and will not fall down.

Also the great Lord teacher, Nàgàrjuna, said
Oh Protector [Buddha], you gave up defilements as well as liberation from the root of habitual tendencies. You achieved nectar through the nature of defilements.

Thus, it is said in the *Question of Upali*:
The bodhisattva's desires, through his great purpose, benefit sentient beings, because his desires make him affectionate to them. So it was said.

Different results appear through the combination of different [causes] [Thus, the cause] of realization of the non-substantial nature [*bdag med*] of phenomena will result in a person never being burdened with attachments. There is no other way to gain the fruition of great bliss. Because of this path of nourishment conduct etc., it is clear that one can achieve perfect bliss. Because would not one agree that similar things transform into what is similar? How could [things] arise from other than what is similar?

Thus *Samvara Tantra* says that:
The buddhas, as well as myself are all heroes.
Therefore, I should practice uniting myself with the supreme deities.
The yogi cannot achieve enlightenment through reflections or imitations.
(folio 56)

Striving diligently for bodhichitta, the *yogi* will become a deity through complete self-abandonment. And not through the torments of asceticism. Only by experiencing bliss can you capture bliss. This (*yogi*) is the future Buddha. This not attained by unnecessary baths and vows, nor is doing difficult ascetic practices necessary, nor ascetic vows. One will not succeed through ascetic practices, but rather one will gain bliss through enjoyment. Buddha said that because of [bodily] forms etc. this completely transformed bliss arises. It is said that in a like manner the cause of the supreme bliss arises from this perfectly transformed touching. And this will bring forth its own result. You may think this contradicts the precepts, and cannot be accepted. But that is not so, for having this special touching [is harmonious with] the precepts, because through it one obtains a [special] result. To those who argue that Buddha has prohibited this, one must reply that there is no problem because the object is only a hindrance to those who Buddha taught can not transform this [touching], as they lack skillful means and wisdom. Because having really attained the result of transformation through the special teaching about touching in the scriptures, how would this contradict the scriptures? Because of this, although one might say that the body is an obstruction, since one has [completely attained the result of the special teaching of the scriptures, they [activities of the body] are transformed. How would this be a contradiction? Because of this, the body is not an obstruction. The object [body] is only a hindrance to those who lacking skillful means and wisdom are completely clinging with desire. They do not know the teachings about total grasping, and they cling to ego. They do not know at all the teachings about how to bring about this transformation of this special touching. Such people grasp completely without understanding this special kind of contact, - touching objects. Thus, objects having been (grasped in this way) may lead to rebirths in the lower realms. Buddha also said:

To a fully ordained monk who is still clinging to phenomena, or one who clings to old traditions, or [has only an] intellectual [interest], one should not show how to make contact with the true nature. Buddha considered it an obstacle for them.

[From the (*Guhyasamàja*].
The path of the ten virtuous actions is for those that give up non-dual wisdom. One should have the wisdom to accept desires. So it has been said.

This is said also in the *Vairocana Tantra*:
Buddha, the great hero, in order to help the Sravakas, when explaining the teachings, taught wisdom without skillful means, when teaching the precepts.(folio 57)

But by totally combining wisdom and skillful means, through diligently searching in this way, through this very special result, one will completely experience the *dharma* of absolute truth [*don dam pai chos kyi de*] (*dharmadhatu*)). Achieving this absolute realization of reality [*go na nyid*], one will not share in even the smallest fault. Thus, by thinking about this in a special way one will gain this unsurpassable result, because one does not have a polluted mind. Through this special mind one will not distinguish between doing what is meritorious and what is non-meritorious, since that distinction does not actually exist in the object.

Aryadeva said that:
The meditation of the bodhisattva will, by the power of all his thoughts [kun rtog], transform all virtue and non-virtue into virtue. Thus it was explained...

This is why the Buddha said that:
If one has faith that everything is like a magical display, for those endowed with faith, everything can be properly enjoyed. They are wrong, however, who claim that those monks who are without faith, who are unworthy to receive alms (because not able to use them correctly, as with this practice) are worthy of enjoying this. (From Samvara Tantra.)

All phenomena have the nature of the sky. Yet, the sky has no characteristics.

In the three realms without exception, all is like a magical display. Like magic, it can be seen and touched, yet it cannot be veridically perceived. In this manner, not having conceptions, the yogi through the practice of *mudrà*, is able to purify all three realms by this special mind.

Thus it is said in the *Assembly of All Gods Tantra* that:
"In this way, one is completely perfected by this union. Otherwise, the foolish are bound by that with which the enlightened one is playing. And it is like a [mere picture of a] lamp. (folio 58)."

Although many methods for doing this are employed in the Vajrayana, the most powerful is the mudra of touch. Through the pleasure experienced in this way, one loses attachment to everything else. But as this equanimity itself is experienced on a higher and higher level it becomes transformed into an experience of absolute nonduality; oneness with being itself. In this way, attachment even to the object of touching is transcended.

"When the madalunga (thorn apple) seed is dyed by the fruit of the laksa (a kind of citron), then its fruit becomes similar to laksa. So when the mind has achieved liberation through bliss it can only dwell in bliss."

Notes
    Snellgrove, David *Indo-Tibetan Buddhism* vol. 1 Boston: Shambhala,1987.
    Bhattacharya, B foreward to the Tattvasamgraha in

Tattvasamgraha of Santaraksita Baroda: Oriental Institute, 1984.

Santaraksita *Tattvasiddhi and Madhyamakalamkara* trans with commentary by Khenchen Palden Sherab Rinpoche and Khentrul Tsewang Dongyal Rinpoche, (with Geshe Lozang Jamspal, Marie-Louise Friquegnon and Arthur Mandelbaum), edited with an introduction by Marie-Louise Friquegnon, forthcoming in Robert Thurman's Buddhist Series, distributed by Columbia University Press.

Descartes, Rene *Principles of Philosophy* trans Thibault, George, trans. Miller, V. R. and Miller, R.P. London: Reidel, 1983.

Ramanuja *Vedantra Sutras* trans. Thibault, George, Delhi: motilal Banarsidass, 1966.

Thurman, Robert *The Central Philosophy of Tibet: A Study and Translation of Jey Tsong Khapa's Essence of True Eloquence* Princeton: Princeton University Press, 1984.

Murkerjee, Madhusree, "Explaining Everything" in *Scientific American* vol. 274, Number 1, 1/96
Mingyur Rinpoche *The Joy of Living* New York: Three Rivers Press, 2008.
Ju Mipham Speech of Delight trans. Thomas Doctor, Ithaca: Snow Lion,2004
Jamgon Mipham The Adornment of the Middle Way trans. Padmakara Translation Group, Boston: Shambhala, 2005

CHAPTER 3

SHANTARAKSHITA, SHANKARA AND THE PROBLEM OF NIHILISM

Sometime within the sixth and eighth century, Buddhist philosopher Shantarakshita and the Vedantin Shankara lived and worked. They do not seem to have debated with each other. (Shantarakshita mentions a Shankara in Tattvasamgraha (3206), but it is not the famous Vedantin. In 3554 comm., Kamalashila identifies this Shankara with the god Shiva.)

If they had met, they could have entered into a dialogue that would have been extremely fruitful for interreligious understanding. Shantarakshita says nothing negative about Advaita Vedanta, the school associated with Shankara, except that they make a slight mistake, that is think that: 1) the Absolute Brahman can be one and permanent and yet assume many forms and 2) all things can be a form of god while beings are still in need of liberation. TS 330-331

Shankara, however, has many criticisms of the Buddhists. 1) He argues that the Buddhists claim that the Buddha taught contradictory and false ideas, namely that a) the external world is real (Theravada) b) all things are composed of mind (Yogacara-Chittamatra) and c) all things are empty in nature. (Madhyamaka) 2) Buddhists are nihilistic, and nihilism cannot be used as a guide to life. 3) Buddhists do not accept an eternal unchangeable reality which forms the basis of the world of appearance. Shankara rejects the momentary collective unconscious or *alaya* of the Yogacaras as an adequate foundation for phenomena. Footnote:A similar summary of Shankara's critique of Buddhism is to be found in Sengaka Mayeda "Shankara and Buddhism" presented at the

International Congress of Vedanta, April 5,1990, Miami University, Oxford, Ohio.

What might Shantarakshita have said in reply to Shankara? First of all, being famous for his cheerfulness, gentleness and conciliatory manner, he would have told Shankara about their points of agreement. He would have been particularly delighted by four of Shankara's views, 1) that one must distinguish between the absolute level which is ineffable,- beyond categories and concepts and the relative level, 2) that language about the absolute is directional. It is not literally true of the absolute, but functions as a finger pointing at the moon. One must not mistake the finger of language for the moon of the true nature. 3) that, as Gaudapada, Shankara's *paramaguru*, (highest teacher) put it, grasping must be completely eliminated in order that enlightenment can be reached. And 4) that the individual self is insubstantial.

To defend Buddhism against Shankara's charges, Shantaraksita would probably have argued in the following way: 1) The Buddha did not really teach in contradictory ways. All of the Buddha's teaching can be understood as a series of finer and finer distinctions concerning the means needed for the elimination of craving. I will now give a rather lengthy discussion of how this historical development is said to have occurred.

Buddhists who adhere to the "second and third turning of the wheel," that is, the Mahayana and the Vajrayana, argue that the Buddha taught in such a way that what he said could be understood in simple terms by his early followers and yet serve as the source of more sophisticated philosophical conclusions in later years. (Similar claims were to be made by Christians about what Christ said to his disciples.) The basic cure for human suffering in all three vehicles, however, was believed to be the elimination of grasping. Without consciousness, there is no suffering. But to eliminate consciousness is to cease to live and although there would then be no suffering, this would be throwing the baby out with the bath water. It is only the craving part of consciousness that causes suffering and hence must go.

As I have said, the history of Buddhism is really the development of how to find more and more subtle ways of eliminating craving. From the very beginning, the source of this craving was identified as the belief in the substantial nature of the individual self. Philosophically, the argument was stated very early in *The Questions of King Milinda*. (Questions of King Milinda, pp.40-45) Just as the word 'chariot' does not stand for a separate entity, but only for a collection of parts such as the axle and wheels, so the name, 'Nagasena', does not stand for a separate entity. It is the name of a collection of *skandhas* or bundles such as a certain series of thoughts, acts of will, sensations, bodily parts and consciousness. One cannot "store up treasure" for such a self for it is never "itself," but constantly changes as its parts change. Once one has eliminated all self-oriented desires, one achieves peace, and suffering is at an end. This is the joy of Nirvana.

As discussed before, many early Buddhists, such as the Vaibhasikas, believed that the external world was composed of atoms, and that these were the real objects of our knowledge. Others, such as the Sautrantikas, believed that while atoms are real their nature is beyond conception. For we never know atoms, which are colorless, tasteless etc., but only sense impressions. But these impressions are caused by atoms.

Madhyamaka philosophers such as Nagarjuna believed that the elimination of craving involves not just no longer clinging to luxuries and loved ones, health and sensual pleasure, but also no longer clinging to one's favorite philosophical point of view. I suppose Nagarjuna, who was surrounded by intellectuals, realized how strong attachments to theories could be. How useful to show no one could cling to a theory about anything!

Nagarjuna's main reason for generating his paradoxes however, was undoubtedly to break down the belief in the existence of objects, because if one does not believe in their nonrelative (ultimate) existence one is less likely to cling to them. It is interesting to note Gaudapada's insistence on the same point.(Gaudapada pp. 161-165)

Nagarjuna's arguments unfold in a manner reminiscent of Zeno's paradoxes. They are directed particularly against the ultimate reality of the world of appearances and the intelligibility of causal relations.

When Nagarjuna first taught in this way, he encountered quite a bit of opposition. He was accused of nihilism, and of denying the central thesis of Buddhism, that is, that suffering is caused by craving. To this he replied in the following way: Reality is beyond our conception. But it appears to us relativistically. Buddha taught on a relative level. There was no other way. But his teaching was designed to lift us above that level. We do this through the elimination of craving. To eliminate craving, however, we must no longer cling to the relative level. We use the teaching as a ladder. When we have reached where we are going, we will throw the ladder away.

But Nirvana (the absolute) and Samsara (the relative) are not separate realms. They are distinguishable in the sense that Nirvana is beyond our relativistic conception. They are not different entities. In Nagarjuna's words:

XXI   "Insoluble "are antinomic' views
         Regarding what exists beyond Nirvana,
         Regarding what the end of this world is,
         Regarding its beginning ...
XXIII   What is identity, and what is difference?
         What is eternity, what noneternity?
         What means eternity and noneternity together?
         What means negation of both issues?
XXIV   Bliss consists in the cessation of all thought,
          In the quiescence of plurality.
          No (separate) reality was preached at all,
          Nowhere and none by Buddha! (Nagarjuna,1995)

This is the philosophical statement of what is said in the "Heart Sutra" of the *Prajanaparamita* where it is proclaimed that "form is emptiness" and "emptiness is form". This view of Nagarjuna's is criticized as nihilistic by Shankara under the name of Sunyavadin or "emptiness" Buddhism. I will return later to the charge of nihilism, but now I wish to explain the charges directed against the

Yogacara which Shankara calls the Vijnavada school.

For Buddhists, everything on the relative level is momentary. (Strictly speaking, the absolute level is neither permanent nor momentary). Mahayana Buddhists, who followed Nagarjuna in denying the reality of atoms, were perplexed about a problem (discussed by Berkeley in the west) about how, if we know everything in terms of our own mental conceptions, we agree from one person to another about what it is we perceive. Jane and John, for example, will both see a cat in front of them.

This problem was taken up in the fourth century by two brothers, Vasubandhu and Asanga. Rejecting materialism, they believed subject and object were both products of ever changing momentary states of consciousness. Since there is no entity such as,the self, subject and object were part of the same flow. For Shantarakshita, subject and object are nevertheless distinguishable but not separable, like waves in the ocean of mind (alaya). Shantarakshita argues for a kind of conceptual dualism on the relative level, for the subject is just that which can never become object. If it did so, it would have to be known by another subject which would entail an infinite regress.

Some momentary states of consciousness produce, in the various skandhas that we call persons, similar experiences because they are produced by similar causal conditions. It is this *alaya*, or momentary states of consciousness, which Shankara argues are an inadequate foundation for reality.

Asanga however, probably believed that the *alaya* is only a useful explanatory tool at the relative level, because consciousness is a concept that can be contrasted with non-consciousness, and since at the absolute level all concepts and distinctions are non-applicable, one could only conclude that the nature of the *alaya* is itself emptiness.

It is this latter position that is endorsed by Shantarakshita in *Madhyamakalankara*. He speaks of himself as riding a chariot holding the bridles of two horses, the Madhyamaka and the Yogacara (Sunyavada and Vijnavada). The Yogacara philosophy is generally true on the relative level, but on closer examination, can be shown to be unintelligible. (His criticisms of the Yogacara philosophy in the Madhyamakalankara analyzed earlier, are very close to Shankara's criticisms of that school. I will return to this later). In the spirit of the development of Buddhist philosophy, Shantarakshita is saying that even clinging to consciousness as real is an obstacle to enlightenment.

Let us now return to Shankara's claim that Buddhism is nihilistic and cannot be a guide to life. First a brief discussion to put the subject in its historical context.

Buddhists commonly refer to Buddhism as "The Middle Way", that is, the way between eternalism and nihilism. By eternalism, they mean the belief that there are eternal, unchanging substances. By rejecting nihilism, they mean not only to reject the view that there is nothing whatever, but also to distinguish themselves from groups like the Carvakas who were moral as well as metaphysical nihilists.

Buddhists, on the other hand, believed in reincarnation, correct moral behavior, religious practices such as prayer and meditation, and what can be loosely called "the sacred". Shankara would question whether or not they had a right to this religious form of life given their philosophy. Shantarakshita would say that on the absolute level he has no philosophy. But on the experiential level, he is convinced that the elimination of craving leads not to a negative or neutral state, but to a state of perfect fulfillment, absolute bliss, the awareness of which is expressed on the relative level through a life of wisdom and compassion.

Shantarakshita discusses this experiential awakening in *Tattvasiddhi*. Since enlightenment does not exist in a separate realm from samsara, it is possible to use cause and effect to alter the mind in such a way that enlightenment happens. Shantarakshita says that just as the seed of a certain bitter fruit can be soaked in milk before planting to produce sweet fruit, so it is possible to use special religious practices to unravel our conceptual awareness and reveal the true nature through non-conceptual awareness. And it just happens to be the case that the true or absolute nature is perceived by the enlightened mind in such a way that the ideas of bliss, wisdom and compassion do not seem totally inappropriate in describing it. This does not seem to be a nihilistic ending of a religious quest. Emptiness is not nothing. 'It' is full of qualities, but these are beyond conception.

The way to the attainment of suchness, among other practices, is living one's life in terms of compassion, loving kindness, and joy in the joy of others. This is not just Shantarakshita's view but was generally accepted by Buddhists. This not only breaks down craving and all forms of selfishness but also the distinction between self and others. With the awareness of the true nature, this attitude is maintained effortlessly. Something about the awareness of the absolute is said to make selfless activities spontaneous. So the philosophy of emptiness can be said to be a way of life.

Shankara had claimed that the momentary *alaya* was an inadequate foundation for reality. As we have already seen, Shantarakshita would agree with him. In *Madhyamalankara* he gives arguments designed to show that whether one says that the mental subject or mental object is one or many, one runs into insurmountable difficulties. On the other hand, he would reject Shankara's criticism of the *alaya,* namely that an unchanging cognizer is needed to account for daily activities like memory or recognition which are subject to residual impressions dependent on place, time and cause. The counter argument would be that to assume they are the memories of an enduring person would be to beg the question and that similarity of the causal conditions from one moment to the next would be sufficient to generate the illusion that they belong to an enduring self.

Nevertheless, the two philosophers agree with the conclusion that the mind cannot be ultimately real. It is not the foundation of reality.

Let us reverse the direction of our investigation at this point, and ask how Shankara might reply to Shantarakshita's criticisms of the Advaita point of view.

1) Can Brahman be one and permanent yet assume many forms? Shantarakshita would say no. But was Shantarakshita replying to an Advaita philosophy that accepted the distinction between the relative and absolute as did Shankara's? Perhaps not. Let us return to the Buddhist distinction between the absolute and the relative. Concepts and distinctions can only be applied on the relative level. The relative level is momentary. But the fourfold negation applies on the absolute level, so strictly speaking, the absolute level is neither permanent, nor changing, nor permanent and changing, nor neither permanent nor changing.

But Shankara also claims that words have only a directional use when applied to the Absolute. They cannot be applied literally to the ineffable. So how can the words `permanent' and 'self' be correctly applied? Does Shankara wish this to mean any more than that in some way the sacred is always there and is the true nature?

2) Shantarakshita questions how all things can be Brahman when beings are in need of liberation. Shankara says we are already Brahman, but our true nature is hidden from us. As someone may mistake a rope for a snake, so we mistake Brahman for the phenomenal world. Shantarakshita similarly believed that since on the absolute level all is the true nature, we are already enlightened. But our true nature is hidden from us as clouds block the sun. We need only remove the obstacles and the true nature will be experienced.

Both the Buddhists and Shankara insist that it is our religious practice that will reveal our true nature to us. Having said this, let me reconsider and look more closely at the concepts of momentariness and permanence as they are used by Shantarakshita and Shankara. My hunch is that the real difference between the two philosophers lies not so much in the strict philosophical implications of what they say, as the differing role these two concepts play in their religious practice. Shankara believes that awareness of the ultimate is facilitated by seeing reality as permanent, unchanging. Shantarakshita believes the opposite. The key seems to be the part played by the importance of the elimination of grasping in the Buddhist system. Shantarakshita is convinced that as long as there is anything left to cling to, anything that is seen as permanent, we will not let go of the relative level and achieve the True Nature. Shankara, however, is convinced that seeing everything as the permanent Lord beyond appearances is the best way to enlightenment. What are we to make of this difference?

One way of understanding it might be to investigate the role of the sacred person in religious experience. It is no secret that the belief in a personal god generates a tremendous amount of emotional force. Although Shankara stressed contemplation more than bhakti (devotion), he wrote devotional hymns. On the relative level, veneration of Ishvara was of great value in achieving liberation. Is there anything like this in Buddhism?

It was not uncommon in Mahayana Buddhism for the *sangha* (community) to be encouraged to see all objects as the body of Buddha, all sounds as the words of Buddha, and all thoughts as the thoughts of Buddha. They were sometimes encouraged to see Buddha in every particle and to see all things as composing Buddha. This visualization was a way of breaking down one's ordinary conceptions and replacing them with a mindfulness leading to awareness of the true nature.

Shantarakshita's fellow teacher in Tibet was Guru Padmasambhava. One of the main teachings of this tantric master was guru yoga. Not only did this involve profound relationship between teacher and student, but the teacher was seen as the embodiment of Buddha, and the phenomenal world itself as the teacher. This visualization did not depend on the actual phenomenal qualities of the teacher. As long as the teacher was at least moderately wise and compassionate, seeing him or her that way facilitated the process of realization of enlightenment. (Similarly Catholics see the priest at the moment of consecration of the bread and wine as embodying Christ). So the emotional force of veneration of Ishvara in Shankara's system does indeed have a counterpart in Shantarakshita's Guru Yoga. The difference is that Shantarakshita combines the skillful means of guru yoga, of seeing reality as the guru, with a simultaneous meditation on the momentariness of the ordinary world.

There are, of course, a lot of unanswered questions. How seriously did Shankara mean his "directional use of language" when applied to Brahman? Which Buddhists contemporary with him was Shankara actually arguing against? Buddhists kept careful records of their debates with those in their own traditions as well as with those in other traditions. Why have I been unable to find Buddhist debates with Shankara? There is only the legend of the debates he had with Dharmakirti over three lifetimes and ending in the sixth century. How well did he know actual Buddhists? If he knew actual Buddhists, might he not have been less hostile? Might he not have realized they were not nihilistic after all? Perhaps someday scholars will be able to answer these questions.

In any case, one biographical note seems to indicate that Shankara, like Shantarakshita, had a similar experience of the compassion of the true nature which transcends all human customs and conventions. For he refused to follow the rules forbidding a *sunyasin* to perform religious rites for a parent. Out of his compassion he fulfilled his childhood promise to his mother and performed the last rites for her sake. When his path was blocked by an untouchable, and the untouchable asked him why he was any less sacred than anyone else, since all is Brahman, Shankara bowed to the untouchable.

CHAPTER 4

CONCLUSION

Shantarakshita and the Great Perfection: Summary

Buddha Sakyamuni. initially presented his philosophy as a cure for human suffering. The key to the cure was to be found in the mind. We cannot control all the conditions in the world which produce pain. But we can control our reactions to it. To use a Buddhist analogy, a man does not try to protect his feet by covering a road with leather. Instead he puts leather shoes on his feet.

But how does one control the mind in such a way as to abolish suffering? The answer was the elimination of grasping. One must give up wanting what one does not have and would like to have, and give up wanting to get rid of what one dislikes. Letting go of grasping puts the mind beyond suffering.

It is not so hard to give up the desire for more and more material possessions. Any reasonable person can see that greed produces suffering. Renunciation of possessiveness toward loved ones is a much harder form of renunciation. But sooner or later most thoughtful people realize that the inevitability of one's own death and that of the beloved make it irrational to make our happiness dependent on continuous contact with them. Philosophical analysis is merely a tool for making this renunciation easier.

Early Buddhists, as discussed previously, accepted the reality of the external world. Many believed it to be composed of atoms. But the existence of atoms was a matter of logic, not experience. It seemed clear that since objects are divisible, they must be divisible into "smallest parts". Some Buddhists argued that since we can never have direct knowledge of atoms, they are beyond conception. All we know are sense impressions which result from interacting atoms. As for the subjective realm, the self was considered to be an illusion generated by one's sense impressions. Internal sensations thoughts, images etc., succeed each other with such rapidity and similarity that they generate the illusion of "same self". But there are no substantial selves. Nor are there substantial objects. Rather there is a temporal river of ever changing atoms, sense impressions, feelings, thoughts etc.

Although changing, the external world was still thought of as real. Later Buddhist philosophers such as Nagarjuna believed it would be useful to show the unreality of atoms because if one does not believe in the reality of a thing, one might be less likely to view it as desirable.

And so the Madhyamaka school of Buddhism was born. A series of arguments resembling Zeno's paradoxes were produced to show the contradictions in the concept of an atom.

In summary:

If an atom is the smallest possible thing it must be indivisible. But to be indivisible the extension of an atom must be zero. Any higher value is divisible. But if the extension is zero, then atoms cannot be the building blocks of the universe, for zero plus zero is always zero. Even the reality of causal relations was called into question. If cause and effect are identical, then everything should happen at once; events cannot be successive, because this would necessitate a separate cause for each effect to bring it about at one specific time rather than another. And cause and effect cannot be different because if the cause precedes the effect it must occupy a different moment in time. So if only the present moment exists, when the cause is present the effect is in a yet nonexistent future, and when the effect is present, the cause is in an already nonexistent past. The cause must act on the effect to bring it about but cannot because they are in separate temporal moments.

The Madhyamaka school was followed by the Chittamatra (or "consciousness only" school) the principal philosophers of which were Asanga and Vasubandhu. These philosophers, while continuing the Buddhist tradition that there is no substantial self, nonetheless argued that the fact of mental experience is inescapable. The mind knows what is given to it in sensation. The mind knows the principles of logic. But if all is mind, how can there be a distinction between subject and object? Their favorite explanation was through an analogy with a dream. In a dream one's mind produces surprising novel experiences. Yet who would deny that the dream object is mental. Why are our experiences alike (person to person) if they are mental? Because they are produced by similar mental habits. The system of mental interdependent co-origination was called the *alaya*.

Shantarakshita unified the Madhyamaka and Chittamatra (also known as Yogacara) points of view. He repeated and extended the ancient arguments against the reality of matter. So it would seem that if reality is not material, it must be mental. Shantarakshita, however, shows that the attempt to link up mental states with mental objects on a one to one basis is hopelessly confused. And so is the attempt to make mind, which is subjectivity, into an object of thought at all. So ultimately mind itself must be understood as being beyond conception.

Shantarakshita speaks of the Madhyamaka and Chittamatra schools as the two chariots, holding the reins of which leads to enlightenment. The correct way to understand the philosophical situation is in terms of both. One must begin with the mental, the impure relativistic knowledge of the world. This is based on distinctions, one term of which cannot be meaningful without its opposite. There is no cold without hot,- no subject without object, - no cause without effect- no existence without nonexistence. The meaning of these terms is relative to a specific context. (To put it in Berkeleyan terms, what is fast to a tortoise is not fast to a hare.) On this level, Shantarakshita could well be termed a pragmatic realist.

Then one must consider that all these distinctions are made relative to a human way of dividing up the world into categories. We think in terms of space and time and we divide up our world into minutes and objects. Thus we have number. We grasp at things; thus we create the illusion of enduring persons who can continue to possess objects. Realizing this, we see all things as an activity of mind. This is the pure relative truth.

But if everything is mind on the relative level, how are we to know there are other minds besides ours? This question was put to Dzigar Kongtrul Rinpoche at a lecture he gave on Shantarakshita's *Madhyamakalankara* September 11, 2011. His answer was that on the relative level we should accept other minds because it is functional to do so. On the ultimate level, of course, all minds are empty of both existence and non-existence.

Finally, we realize we know mind inauthentically, that is as object, rather than subject. But if mind is really awareness and can never be an object, we can never know it in terms of categories. The nature of mind is itself beyond conception. It is emptiness. That is the absolute truth.

To reiterate, it is important to realize that the absolute and the relative are not two separate realms. The relative is just the absolute seen from the relative point of view. This is what is meant in the "Heart Sutra" when it is said that "Form is emptiness, emptiness is form". The further the mind progresses in giving up distinctions, categories etc. the closer it comes to absolute awareness. So the relative is not the enemy of the absolute, but the way in which it can be realized. This is the point of the *Tattvasiddhi*.

Shantarakshita and Dzogchen

To return to the early Buddhist conception of Nirvana, while indeed the elimination of craving does produce the absence of suffering, and even a kind of peace, why should the bodhisattvas speak of it as being so blissfully wonderful? Why doesn't the extinction of desire lead to a kind of stoic calm rather than such perfect joyful fulfillment? The answer to this question provides the *raison d'etre* of Dzogchen, the highest teaching of the Vajrayana.

According to Dzogchen there is something about the true nature that lends itself to being experienced in a way that is productive of perfect happiness,— a happiness that joyfully overflows into wise and compassionate activity. This is not something that is provably true. It is the result of a perspectival shift- leading to an experience of a special kind. But although it is special in terms of ordinary sentient beings, it is the normal, natural way of experiencing reality. Dzogchen practitioners believe we are prevented from having this experience because of the grasping nature of ordinary mind. Failing to understand the inherent emptiness of all things, we grasp at them. Failing to get what we want, we become angry, jealous, fearful, full of hate. Our perception is distorted and impoverished. Through the practice of selflessness, loving kindness, compassion and meditation, these poisons are overcome. As the mind relaxes it is prepared to learn to see in a new way.

Since mind is simply the relative side of the true nature, it can be transformed in such a way as to be a pure reflection of the absolute. To do this, special skills are necessary. These are the inner tantric practices: *maha, anu* and *ati yoga.*

The outer tantras involve external practices such as breathing, fasting or control of diet etc. The inner practices are forms of mental training. They are complex, but briefly they are described as follows by Khenchen Palden Sherab Rinpoche:

"...according to Mahayoga, we should feel deeply [during the visualization (creation) stage of meditation)] that the whole world is a celestial mansion, and that every single being it contains is a deity. Whatever thoughts crop up in our head should be seen as manifestations of wisdom, and any conversations we have or any sounds we hear should be experienced as mantra.
In the Anuyoga Tantras [meditation], our *skandhas* [body, feelings, sensations, thoughts, consciousness] are seen as a microcosm of the external world...[A]ccording to Anuyoga, the external world is really a reflection of our own skandhas, and not an independent reality as such...

According to Atiyoga, there is not even a speck of dust or a single atom that does not embody primordial purity [enlightenment]...According to this view, if we are able to realize the authentic condition of how we are right now, we can become enlightened on the spot... (Khenchen Palden Sherab 2009. Chap. 13)

Now to return to the *Tattvasiddhi*. Although this work does not mention the three inner tantras by name, their use is implied in this work. And Shantarakshita in Tibet worked hand in glove with the great Dzogchen teacher, Guru Padmasambhava. Because on the ultimate level, we are already considered to be enlightened, on the relative level, it is possible to make use of certain causal conditions which produce special results leading to enlightenment. Having already purified the mind of the poisons of ignorance and fear, anger and hatred, jealousy and attachment, and, through the practice of philosophy realized the emptiness of all forms, the practitioner is ready to use the manure of the city in the farmyards of the countryside. The practice of the six *paramitas*, generosity, effort, patience, morality, mindfulness and wisdom have ensured that this "manure" will not be misused.

What is this "manure"? It is the worldly practices involving desire which were considered necessary to be renounced in traditional monastic Buddhism. Chief among these is sexual union. In the *Tattvasiddhi,* referred to as "touch," it becomes an experience leading to enlightenment.

Shantarakshita, of course, is not referring to sexual union as it is practiced by ordinary people. It has to be transformed by the mind. It must be free of attachment and dualistic thinking. It becomes, through this transformation, a living symbol of the unity of form and emptiness, of wisdom and compassion.

Why is this great mudra or "great seal" so essential in the production of awareness of the true nature, of enlightenment itself? Shantarakshita argues that on the relative level, like causes produce like effects. The result of enlightenment is a state of ecstatic bliss. One can never prepare the way for this through painful ascetic practices. They will only sadden and confuse the mind. The joy of union, however, is in some ways similar to awareness of the true nature. In this joy, all distinctions seem to disappear. Lover and beloved seem to flow into each other. Subject and object as distinct entities seem to melt away.

Fear and grasping cause clinging, and thus more and more sorrow. But in the great seal, the partners visualize each other as god and goddess, form and emptiness, wisdom and compassion. The experience of union becomes a meditation on the true nature. So the great seal becomes a special cause productive of enlightenment. The absence of craving precludes the onset of suffering. The great seal establishes the yogi (male) and yogini (female) more and more firmly in the awareness of the true nature. But this practice is one that goes beyond sensation to reveal the bliss of wisdom rather than emotion.

In the *Tathvasiddhi*, Shantarakshita offers a logical argument for the possibility of the attainment of enlightenment. But of course, as he admits, it cannot be proved that anyone has actually achieved enlightenment in this way. This is a "try and see" procedure for those who have already achieved a high degree of realization through the elimination of poisons and the practice of virtue.

Why can it not be proved that anyone has ever reached enlightenment? This brings us back to the nature of Dzogchen. And I believe Wittgensteinian perspectivism has provided us with a conceptual framework for understanding Dzogchen.

In the *Philosophical Investigations*, Wittgenstein illustrates his ideas about perspectives through the duck/rabbit example. Given a certain illustration, one can see it as either a duck or a rabbit. Sometimes people can only see the duck or only the rabbit. If they can only see one, we might call them "aspect blind".

In his book *Philosophy of Art* , Virgil Aldrich uses this example of the duck/rabbit to illustrate problems about what one sees when one sees a picture. There is, for Aldrich, a root sense of a thing. But we never know things in this root sense. Things always appear to us under one aspect or another. (Aldrich, 1963)

Take a painting, for example. If the painting is large, men moving it may very likely ignore its beauty and concentrate on its physical aspects; its weight and shape. An art lover watching them move may be oblivious to its physical aspects but enchanted by its grace and proportion, its aesthetic aspects. Someone who could not see the painting from this aesthetic perspective, we might consider "aspect blind". Since perception of beauty is a normal human ability, we might ask why this person's perception is blocked. Perhaps if the viewer hates religion, and the painting has a religious subject, this hatred may make the viewer incapable of appreciating the painting's grace and dynamism. Removal of this hatred might free the "aesthetic eye" of a beholder.

Virgil Aldrich's application of Wittgensteinian perspectivism to art could be extended, to psychology and morality as well. Autistic children, because of fear or other causes, may be unable to see other people as people. They are incapable of taking the psychological perspective, Great kindness and patience in working with these children may occasionally result in a lifting of the barriers to the normal psychological point of view. Holding the hand of another child, putting on the clothes of another, may all be learning devices which prepare the way for the interpersonal psychological experience.

Moral awareness may also be blocked in some people. The ethical point of view, considered so normal, may not be part of the experience of criminals described by the police as moral idiots. Such people do not knowingly choose to perform wrong actions rather than right. They see the world in terms of practical expediency and not in terms of morality at all. They fail to see the moral picture.

So far I have described a series of perspectives, physical, aesthetic, psychological and moral. Perspectives are neither true nor false. At most they can be considered apt or inapt. It is true that certain things lend themselves to be perceived in certain ways more easily than others. Monet's water lily paintings are easier to see as aesthetic objects than a toaster. But we couldn't prove that someone who saw a toaster as beautiful was wrong. As Descartes pointed out, we do not know that the being we see walking outside the window wearing a coat and hat is a person like ourselves and not an automaton, yet it seems more reasonable to assume so.

The Dzogchen masters are claiming that there is an additional perspective we can take toward being and that this perspective is indeed more apt than any other. They cannot describe this perspective to those who do not share it, any more than we could describe the aesthetic perspective (or moral perspective) to someone incapable of taking these points of view. Similarly, to those of us incapable of taking the enlightened perspective, such a perspective seems incommunicable.

The analysis, however, should not be pushed too far. Buddhists claim that enlightenment is in principle beyond conception, because all conceptions involve distinctions. And the state of enlightenment is beyond distinction. On the aesthetic level one can distinguish between paintings that are static and those which are dynamic. But one could not distinguish enlightenment qualities, except in terms of the varying effects of the meditation on the meditator. Further, with all other perspectives, there is a subject and an object. The egolessness of the state of enlightenment however, precludes dualistic awareness. The distinction between subject and object has been dissolved.

Thus Dzogchen masters insist that the enlightenment state is not nothingness, but is filled with qualities. Here the rational mind must leave off because we cannot imagine a fullness of being that is beyond distinctions. Perhaps when we reach such a level we will understand.

What reason do we have to suppose such a level is reachable,- that there is such a level at all? To have reason to believe in the existence of enlightenment, there must be points of access to it long before it has been actually reached. This is called by some Buddhist writers the *tathatagarbha*, or seed of enlightenment. There are examples of the bliss of enlightenment in ordinary experience, such as the objectless joy of the happy child, and in adult life, those precious moments of tranquility when one feels at one with the universe, or even as Karl Jasper's suggests, when one has gone through a tragic experience and been strengthened by it. Such intimations serve as assurance that the search for enlightenment is not the pursuit of an imaginary goal, and why the achievement of this goal should lead to bliss rather than indifference. Further evidence is provided by the aura of radiant happiness and compassion of the great teachers.

The most the philosopher can do is suggest that Dzogchen constitutes a philosophically coherent view of religious experience, one in which a perspectival shift has been substituted for faith in doctrines. Whether or not that shift is possible, or whether reality is objectively of such a nature as to be experienced this way must be decided for themselves by those who set out on this path.

Shantarakshita argues for the plausibility of such an attainment. His evidence for its actual realization rests on the testimony of great yogis and yoginis who have said they have experienced this great happiness. Modest as always, he never claims to have reached it himself.

Shantarakshita's Significance

I began this study with the claim that Shantarakshita stands at the culminating point of a tradition, in a way similar to Immanuel Kant. There is indeed a striking similarity between the two philosophers. Both divide knowledge into the absolute (noumenal) and relative (phenomenal) levels, considering the absolute as a regulative principle rather than an object of knowledge. Both rejected skepticism, sense data theory and ultimate idealism.

There is even a similarity in their vision of the noumenal in a religious way. In the last analysis in *The Critique of Pure Reason*, Kant refuses to distinguish between substance, the transcendental self and God. Kant sees God as the ultimate unifying principle, itself unknowable, which unifies substance and soul:

"...if I think of a being as existing which corresponds to a mere idea, and a transcendental one, I ought not to admit the existence of such a being by itself, because no concepts through which I can conceive any object definitely can reach it, and the conditions of the objective validity of my concepts are excluded by the idea itself. The concepts of reality, of substance, even of causality, and those of necessity in existence, have no meaning that could determine any object, unless they are used to make the empirical knowledge of an object possible. They may be used, therefore, to explain the possibility of things in the world of sense, but not to explain the possibility of a universe itself, because such a hypothesis is outside the world and could never be an object of possible experience. I can, however, admit perfectly well such an inconceivable Being, being an object of a mere idea, relative to the world of sense, though not as existing by itself."(Kant,1961 pp. 399-600)

For Shantarakshita, the attainment of emptiness is the goal of religion (*dharma*). Unlike Kant, however, he sees the tantra as the "skillful means" needed to immerse oneself in non-conceptual awareness. Kant would have rejected the possibility of any awareness of the noumenal, because for him concepts were inescapable. And as Kant responded critically to Berkeley, Shantarakshita rejects, on the ultimate level, the vision of world as idea. His view that nirvana and samsara are two different perspectives is suggestive of Spinoza.

His criticism of a necessary connection between cause and effect and his affirmation of the bundle theory of the self are similar to David Hume. His theory of language will be echoed later in the work of Wittgenstein. His idea that the mind is dependent on the "power of another", that is, on habitual tendencies, is suggestive of views by some contemporary cognitive scientists that the brain is similar to a computer program which determines our mental states and activities. Contemporary cognitive science has not yet offered us a way out of the matrix. If Shantarakshita's vision is correct, he does. He is truly a philosopher for all seasons.

Notes:
Aldrich, Virgil *Philosophy of Art* Englewood Cliffs: Prentice Hall, 1963.

Kant, Immanuel *Critique of Pure Reason, "The Elements of Transcendentalism, Appendix"* trans. Max Muller. New York, Dophin Macmillan, 1961.

Glossary

Abhidharma—words of the Buddha, forming one third of the Tripitaka. Teachings on discriminating knowledge by analyzing elements of experience and investigations into the nature of existing things.

alaya—ground consciousness which in Cittamatra sparks all awareness.

amrita—nectar

arhat— "foe destroyer." A disciple of Buddha who has attained Nirvāna after conquering the four klesas (defilements), and has 'conquered' (hata) his 'enemies'(ari).

Bhagavan— Buddha, (in Hinduism, Vishnu.)

bodhicitta— "awakened state of mind." The aspiration to attain enlightenment for the sake of all beings. Wisdom and compassion.

Carvaka—materialist, nihilist philosopher.

Cittamatra—mind-only school of Buddhist philosophy.

Dergey—an edition of the Tibetan Buddhist canon.

dewa chenpo— great bliss.

Dharmadhatu— "realm of phenomena." The nature of mind and phenomena, which lies beyond arising, dwelling, and ceasing. The suchness in which dependent origination and emptiness are inseparable.

dharmakaya— the body of enlightened qualities. One of the three kayas, devoid of constructs.

Great Ascetic—Buddha

great emptiness—ultimate reality beyond conception

gunas— qualities.

Hinayana—vehicles focusing on the four noble truths and the twelve links of dependent origin for individual liberation.

Inter-dependent co-origination—The interdependence of all things at each moment of time, arising within the system of cause and effect.

Isvara —the Lord (Hindu).

kalpa—a very long period of time—four thousand three hundred and twenty millions of years.

Kasyapa—the disciple of the Buddha who inherited leadership of the sangha.

Kaya—the three kaya: dharmakaya, sambhogakaya , and nirmanakaya, are ground as essence, nature, and expression; as path are bliss, charity, and nonthought; and as fruition are the three kayas of buddhahood.

kriya yoga—first of the three outer tantras, emphasizing purity of action and cleanliness.

kun tags—mental exaggerations

lata—vine.

Madhyamaka—school of Mahayana Buddhism that stresses emptiness.

Mahayana—great vehicle, course, or journey. Major division of Buddhism in which one strives toward Buddha rather than an arhat.

mandala— "center and surrounding." Symbolic representation of a tantric deity's realm of existence, a ritually protected space

Manjushri— bodhisattva of wisdom.

Mimamsa —a school of Hindu philosophy that held that the universe was an external container of the Vedas.

mudra—seal; hand gesture ritual.

Nirmanakaya— emanational body of Buddha.

Naiyayika— the logic school of Buddhism.

Nyaya –Vaibhasika— the combined logic and atomistic Hindu schools.

Paramita— perfection; the six or ten virtues of Buddhism: generosity, moral conduct, renunciation, wisdom, energy, patience, truthfulness, determination, loving-kindness, equanimity.

Pitaka—basket; there are 3 baskets of Buddhism: Sutra pitaka (sayings of Buddha,) Vinaya (monastic law,) and abhidharma pitaka (philosophy.)

prakriti—nature

pramana—source of proof: direct perception, inference, and trustworthy testimony or scripture.

Pratyekabuddha— "solitary Buddha,"one who reaches Awakening without help and does not preach to others.

probandum— conclusion.

probans— premises.

Pudgala (gan zag)— a person.

rigpa— knowledge.

rupakaya— the realm of forms comprising the Sambhogakaya and nirmanakaya.

sadhana—tantric or esoteric practice.

Sankhya —a school of Hindu philosophy that held that all phenomena came from prakrti (nature.)

Sarvastivadins—members of the All-Exists school of Buddhism, that accepted the existence of past, present, and future; and denied the reality of self-consciousness.

Sautrantika — "adherents of the Sutras." early school of Buddhism, that believed reality is indirectly known through mental object, and Sutra is atomistic in nature.

sems tsam pa— mind-only school.

Siddha— "accomplished one." Buddhist adept who has attained siddhi.

Siddhi—power or ability.

sloka—verse.

sravaka —Disciple of the Buddha who seeks to be an arhat.

Sugata— "Blissfully Gone," an enlightened being, particularly the historical Buddha Shakyamuni.

Sunyata—Emptiness, without substantial independence, fundamental notion in Mahayana conception of Ultimate Reality.
Sutra—Collection of the Buddha's discourses

tala— palmyra tree.

tantra— a mystical treatise; Esoteric Buddhist or Hindu tradition and texts.

Tathagatagarbha—"Womb or embryo of the Buddha." Innate potential for Buddhahood.

tatura—cotton plant

tendrel—system of independant co-origination.

Vaibhasika—Buddhist philosophical school that held that all things are composed of atoms.

Vaisesika — A Hindu philosophical school that believed reality to be composed of atoms.

Vajrayana— "Vajra vehicle." A form of Mahayana that uses special techniques for the attainment of enlightenment.

Vasubhandu—Fourth century Buddhist Mind-Only philosopher.

Vinaya— Monastic rules of conduct.

yana— vehicle or path.

Yogacara — "Practice of yoga." Major Mahayana school emphasizing the nature of consciousness.

Bibliography

Aldrich, Virgil. *Philosophy of Art* Englewood Cliffs: Prentice Hall, 1963.

Anacker, Stefan. *Seven Works of Vasubandhu: The Buddhist Psychological Doctor* Delhi: Motilal Banarsidass, 1998.

Bhattacharyya, B. Foreword to the Tattvasamgraha in *Tattvasamgraha of Shantarakshita* Baroda: Oriental Institute, 1984.

Blumenthal, James. *The Ornament of the Middle Way: A Study of the Madhyamaka Thought of Shantarakshita*. Ithaca, New York: Snow Lion, 2004

Dreyfus, Georges and McCintock, Sara eds. *The Svatantrika-Prasangika Distinction: what difference does a difference make?* Boston: Wisdom, 2003

Doctor, Thomas, and *Speech of Delight: Mipham's Commentary on Shantarakshita's Ornament of the Middle Way:* Ithaca: Snow Lion, 2004

Dreyfus, Georges B. *Recognizing Reality: Dharmakirti's Philosophy and Its Tibetan Interpretations*. Albany: SUNY Press, 1997.

Duckworth, Douglas S. *Jamgon Mipam: His Life and Teaching*. Boston: Shambhala, 2011

Mipam on Buddha Nature: The Ground of the Nyingma Tradition. Albany: SUNY Press,2008

Dudjom Rinpoche *The Nyingma School of Tibetan Buddhism*. Trans. Gyume Dorje and Matthew Kapstein. Boston: Wisdom Publications, 1991.

Friquegnon, M and Dinnerstein, N. eds. *Studies in the Yogachara Madhyamaka of Santaraksita*, New York: Global Scholarly Publications, 2012
Gupta, Bina *An Introduction to Indian Philosophy* New York: Routledge, 2012

Hopkins, Jeffrey. *Emptiness in the Mind-Only School of Tibetan Buddhism. Dynamic Responses to Dzong-ka-ba's The Essence of Eloquence, vol. 1.* Berkeley: University of California Press, 1999.

— *Reflections on Reality: The Three Natures and Non-Natures in the Mind-Only School. Dynamic Responses to Dzong-ka-ba's The Essence of Eloquence, vol. 2.* Berkeley: University of California Press, 2002.

Ichigo, Masamichi. *Madhyamakalamkara of Shantarakshita with his own commentary or Vrtti and with the Sub commentary or Panjika of Kamalashila. Kyoto: Buneido,* 1985. *Madhyamakalamkara* trans. Masamichi, I.

Ichigo, Masamichi. Gomez, Luis O and Silk, Jonathan A. *Literature of the Great Vehicle: Three Mahayana Buddhist Texts* (Michigan Studies in Buddhist Literature). Centers for South and Southeast Asia, 1999.

Isayeva, Natalia. *Shankara and Indian Philosophy* Albany: SUNY Press, 1993.

Jha, Ganganatha. *The Tattvasamgraha of Shantarakshita with the Commentary of Kamalashila. 2 vols.* Reprint, Delhi: Motilal Banarsidass.

Kant, Immanuel. *The Critique of Pure Reason* trans. Muller, F.Max Garden City: Dolphin Macmillan, 1961.

Kapstein, Matthew. *The Fallacies of Personalistic Vitalism* Journal of Indian Philosophy. Dordrecht Holland: D. Reidel Vol 17 March, 1989 pp. 43-59.

Lopez Jr., Donald. *A Study of Svatantrika* Ithaca: Snow Lion, 1987.

Mingyur Rinpoche, Yongey *The Joy of Living* New York: Three Rivers Press , 2008.

Mipham Shantarakshita's Madhyamakalankara with Commentary Padmakara Translation Group . Boston: Shambhala,2005

Murti, M.R.V. *The Central Philosophy of Buddhism.* London: Allen and Unwin, 1955.

Nagarjuna. *The Fundamental Wisdom of the Middle Way.* translation and commentary by Garfield, Jay L. Oxford: Oxford University Press, 1995. Potter, Karl. *Presuppositions of Indian Philosophies.* Engelwood Cliffs: Prentice Hall, 1963.

Ramanuja, *The Vedanta Sutra.* trans. Thibault, George. Delhi: Motilal Banarsidass, 1966.

Shantarakshita. *Tattvasamgraha. vols. 1&2.* trans. Jha, Ganganatha Delhi: Motilal Banarsidass, 1937

The Adornment of the Middle Way: Shantarakshita's Madhyamakalankara with Commentary by Jamgon Mipham. Padmakara Translation Group. Boston: Shambhala, 2005.

Sarachcandra, Edirivira R. *"From Vasubandhu to Shantarakshita" Journal of Indian Philosophy vol.4 no. 1/2 Sept./`Dec., 1976 pp.70-107.*

Siderits, Mark *Buddhism As Philosophy.* Hackett: Indianapolis, 2007.

Sherab (Rinpoche), Khenchen Palden *Ceaseless Echoes of Great Silence: A Commentary on the Heart Sutra* trans. Dongyal (Rinpoche),Ven. Khenpo Tsewang Boca Raton: Sky Dancer, 1993.

Sherab, Khenchen Palden Rinpoche *Turning the Wisdom Wheel of the Nine Golden Chariots* trans. Ven. Traleg Kyabgon Rinpoche, Sidney Center, New York: Dharma Samudra,2009
Sherab (Rinpoche), Khenchen Palden and Dongyal (Rinpoche), Khentrul Tsewang.
The *Tattvasiddhi and the Madhyamakalamkara of Shantarakshita with Commentaries.* Trans. Sherab (Rinpoche), Khenchen Palden, Dongyal (Rinpoche), Khentrul Tsewang, Friquegnon, Marie and Mandelbaum, Arthur. forthcoming Buddhist Series ed. Robert Thurman, Columbia University Press.
Opening the Wisdom Door of the Madhyamaka School by Khenchen Palden Sherab Rinpoche and Khenpo Tsewang Dongyal Rinpoche. New York: Dharma Samudra, 2007.

Opening the Clear Vision of the Yogacara School by Khenchen Palden Sherab Rinpoche and Khenpo Tsewang Dongyal Rinpoche. New York: Dharma Samudra, 2007

Splendid Presence of the Great Guhyagarbha: Opening the Wisdom Door of the King of All Tantras by Khenchen Palden Sherab Rinpoche and Khenpo Tsewang Dongyal Rinpoche. New York: Dharma Samudra, 2011.

Smart, Ninian *Doctrine and Argument in Indian Philosophy* London, 1964

Snellgrove, David *Indo-Tibetan Buddhism vols 1&2* Boston: Shambhala, 1987
The Cowherd *Moonshadows: Conventional Truth in Buddhist Philosophy.* New York: Oxford University Press, 2011
Thurman, Robert A.F. *Tsong Khapa's Speech of Gold in the Essence of True Eloquence: Reason and Enlightenment in the Central Philosophy of Tibet.* Princeton: Princeton University Press, 1978

Westerhoff, Jan *Nagarjuna's Madhyamaka Oxford:* Oxford University Press, 2009

Nagarjuna's *Vigrahavyavartani: The Dispeller of Disputes* (translation and commentary) New York: Oxford University Press, 2010

Wittgenstein, Ludwig *Philosophical Investigations* trans. Anscombe, G. New York: Macmillan, 1953

Index

About the Author

Marie Friquegnon is Professor of Philosophy and of Asian Studies at William Paterson University. She earned her PhD in Philosophy at New York University. She is the author of *On Shantarakshita, and Reflections on Childhood.* She edited and co-translated with Khenchen Palden Sherab Rinpoche and Khentrul Tsewang Dongyal Rinpoche Santaraksita's *Tattvasiddhi and Madhyamakalankara* with Rinpoches' commentaries (forthcoming Columbia University). She edited with Noe Dinnerstein Studies in the *Yogacara Madhyamaka of Santaraksita,* and with Raziel Abelson, *Clarity and Vision and Ethics for Modern Life.* She is currently at work on a translation/commentary of Santaraksita's *Madhyamakalankara Vritti.,* a collection of essays, *Buddhism and Philosophy* and an intellectual memoir *Finding Santaraksita.* She is editing with Benjamin Abelson, a collection of Raziel Abelson's essays, *Window to Truth.* and a collection of readings *Great Disputes in Philosophy.* She is a student of Khentrul Tsewang Dongyal Rinpoche.

.